CITIZENSHIP

D1196384

PASSPORT

5013865

CITIZENSHIP

DIMITRY KOCHENOV

The MIT Press | Cambridge, Massachusetts | London, England

This book was set in Chaparral Pro by Toppan Best-set Premedia Limited. Printed and bound in the United States of America.

Library of Congress Cataloging-in-Publication Data

Names: Kochenov, Dimitry, 1979- author.
Title: Citizenship / Dimitry Kochenov.
Description: Cambridge, MA : The MIT Press, [2019] | Series: The MIT Press Essential Knowledge series | Includes bibliographical references and index.
Identifiers: LCCN 2019005626 | ISBN 9780262537797 (paperback : alk. paper)
Subjects: LCSH: Citizenship.
Classification: LCC JF801.K64 2019 | DDC 323.6—dc23 LC record available at https://lccn.loc.gov/2019005626

10   9   8   7   6   5   4   3   2   1

E pluribus unum is an alchemist's promise;
out of liberal pluralism no oneness can come.

—Michael Walzer

CONTENTS

SERIES FOREWORD

The MIT Press Essential Knowledge series offers accessible, concise, beautifully produced pocket-size books on topics of current interest. Written by leading thinkers, the books in this series deliver expert overviews of subjects that range from the cultural and the historical to the scientific and the technical.

In today's era of instant information gratification, we have ready access to opinions, rationalizations, and superficial descriptions. Much harder to come by is the foundational knowledge that informs a principled understanding of the world. Essential Knowledge books fill that need. Synthesizing specialized subject matter for nonspecialists and engaging critical topics through fundamentals, each of these compact volumes offers readers a point of access to complex ideas.

Bruce Tidor
Professor of Biological Engineering and Computer Science
Massachusetts Institute of Technology

Few concepts are as seemingly self-evident and at the same time as deeply misunderstood as citizenship. Citizenship is ancient, yet it is as appealing today as it was in the days of Aristotle: political participation, emancipation, and belonging to a community—all good things and comfortably familiar, like well-thumbed paperbacks. Flags, elections, passports, and glorious histories aside, citizenship seems almost boring—what could there be left to write a book about? A great deal, it will turn out, as much remains concealed behind the self-evident and self-explanatory: as much as citizenship is an instrument of political empowerment and positive identity building, it is a calculated tool to tame populations, local and foreign, into complacency and to uphold the status quo of local and global injustice. When examined closely, citizenship reveals itself as a historically violent and ultimately totalitarian status of premodern nature, both rigid to an extreme and capriciously random in how it is assigned, leaving no room for choice or merit, glorying in its sexism and racism. Having been so essential to citizenship through its history, these characteristics have only recently started to fade with overwhelming reluctance over the last few decades, leaving much of citizenship devoid of meaning. As a vestige of the world predating the ideals of equality, justice, and merit, which move us today, citizenship finds itself in a truly difficult place; and once you scratch the surface of the notion, the official narrative of political emancipation rarely conceals its flaws.

However incongruous to the modern world, citizenship is very well integrated into it. It plays a fully internalized, crucial role in the life of modern democracies, and is embellished with dignity and reason when it is taught. The most fascinating feature of citizenship is this deep contradiction between its essence and its purpose on the one hand, and its reputation on the other. The story of citizenship is as much a story of flattering the pride of those who are proclaimed to "belong"—a tale of liberation, dignity, and nationhood—as it is one of complacency, hypocrisy, and blunt domination, all dressed up as agency and the pursuit of the common good. It's an efficient way to split societies down the middle, leaving scars and divisions that are very difficult to heal. Citizenship is known to be a "good thing," and a bad citizen is less deserving of compassion, understanding, or a voice. Indeed, those proclaimed "bad citizens" end up ignored or exiled and deprived of their status. Citizenship is a powerful instrument to reinforce popular prejudices and create new ones.

Nonetheless, at the core of modern citizenship lies a most commendable ideal of equality and dignity that can be traced back to St. Paul: the abstract concept is an idealistic proclamation, masking the actual differences between people and their passions, abilities, and aspirations. Citizenship is first of all a tool for simplifying the world. After its astonishing effectiveness in rendering people governable, what has made citizenship so popular and underpins its global reach must undoubtedly be the role it plays as the uniform shorthand for simplifying the overwhelming diversity and complexity of human societies. This is indeed a glorious proliferation. From the minuscule proportion of the population of Aristotle's Athens to the absolute majority of the seven billion of the Earth's population today, citizenship has spread. A multitude of factors explain this, from the gradual rise of individualism and the global proliferation of nationhood and statehood—essentially dependent precisely on citizenship—to the attractive ideas of dignity, equality, and human worth applied to strictly separated groups of individuals around the world, hundreds of times over. These ideals disappear, unfortunately, once two or more societies are considered, as opposed to only one. Proclaimed a servant of the great ideals, citizenship is a very effective abstract legal tool to justify essentially random violence, humiliation, and exclusion.

This book is about what citizenship is, what it entails, how it came about, and how its role in the world has been changing. Crucially, it is not an account aiming to glorify the concept no matter what: what follows is a critical introduction to the idea, one that penetrates deeper than citizenship's most popular clichés, which rarely delve

Citizenship is first of all
a tool for simplifying
the world.

beyond presenting it as an indispensable element of political activity, with the political rights of citizens as its defining characteristic. As this book will demonstrate, walking down this well-worn path would miss citizenship's core features, which would be a pity in a work this concise. Accounts of the glories and dignity of citizenship are everywhere, yet it is the arbitrariness, violence, and servility attending citizenship—coupled with its war on individuality and its sanctification in the fight for the preservation of the status quo, no matter which society and time we are talking about—that we must focus on when we interrogate it. Add to this citizenship's inherent racism, its deep and chronic exclusion of women, and its upholding and reinforcing of class divisions between the haves and have-nots, and it becomes clear why citizenship is at a crossroads today: the ideals it emerged to defend have little to do with all that drives the thinking behind a good society in the contemporary world. As a result, citizenship is changing at an increasing pace and we will trace the most significant among the vectors of this ongoing change. Citizenship's relevance in a contemporary world that purports leaving behind a heritage glorifying servility, racism, sexism, and arbitrary exclusion—citizenship's core features—is far from clear, or at least not self-evident.

In addition to a couple of decades of reading about citizenship and writing on it for strictly professional audiences, this book also draws on my constant engagement with the subject as a global lawyer with intimate familiarity with the relevant disputes, from the European Union to the Chagos Archipelago in the middle of the Indian Ocean. Although written by a lawyer, it is not a legal account of the black-letter nitty-gritty based on any concrete legal system past or present. Instead, it is a *tour d'horizon* of the basic elements of the concept of citizenship and key stages in its development, which are generalizable beyond any concrete legal system. This generalization is the core benefit of this work, since it brings to light crucial features of citizenship that would remain invisible at the scale of the individual state. The global outlook allows distillation of citizenship's essential features without falling into the trap of nationalist assumptions. This has a significant added value, at times presenting a seemingly very familiar notion in a radically different light.

D. K.
Royal Netherlands Institute in Rome, July 2018

KEY ELEMENTS OF THE CONCEPT

When Herr Händel, the composer of music for King George I, was made into Mr. Handel in 1727, naturalizations were uncommon. Handel was admitted into the subjecthood of the British king by a special Act of Parliament, which was the only procedure available at the time. However rare, naturalization stories are well known from the past. Another composer, signor Giovanni Battista Lulli, a subject of the Grand Duke of Florence, in 1661 became the powerful French nobleman Jean-Baptiste de Lully, in recognition of his friendship with and music making for the Sun King. The most exceptional were the kings and queens themselves, for whom subjecthood could not exist as such, of course. George I is a perfect example: he was an illustrious German Elector of Hannover until several years prior to Händel's naturalization and was known to not be a lover of all things English.

The absolute majority of others—those not boasting royal blood—were definitely much less fortunate: as the official story goes, citizenship, the status of fully belonging to any community, used to be assigned strictly and for life. The cases where citizenship was changed were thus very few. However counterintuitive this might sound in the context of today's globalized world, 350 years after the Florentine Lulli received his French papers, the deep exceptionalism of status change remains. Even though many of us know a naturalized American, have heard of an Olympian switching countries, or of a millionaire taking up the citizenship of St Kitts and Nevis, all the cases of naturalization in the world combined would still amount to less than 2 percent of the world's population.[1] These are thus almost within a negligible margin of error and, although telling, cannot possibly supply a solid basis for a full story.

This book will take a bigger picture, looking at the status of citizenship enjoyed by all, including those—an overwhelming majority—who never changed it. We will consider how and why the status of citizenship is extended, which functions it serves, and who is left behind when such statuses are distributed. We then move on to the rights the status of citizenship is usually associated with, putting emphasis on the most important rights present in all states all over the world. We will especially focus on the right to enter the state issuing the status of citizenship and the right to work and reside there, as well as other rights and freedoms, which are more context-specific and less universal, including social entitlements, and meaningful participation in elections. From rights we will move to duties, which the holders of the status of citizenship are usually expected to perform, such as, especially, the obligation to be a "good citizen" and to love the motherland, however wanting it is. The final chapter covers the politics of citizenship, coupled with the analysis of the role that political rights play in the story of the assignment and enjoyment of the status of citizenship. The remaining pages of the introduction explain very briefly how all these elements of the citizenship puzzle—status, rights, duties, politics—interconnect and evolve. A concise aside delves into the relationship between the status of citizenship and identity, aiming to caution against reading too much into this tandem, which could be a false friend, although composed of really solemn words, seemingly ripe with meaning.

Let us look at each of these building blocks in more detail before we turn to each of the four essential parts of citizenship in specific chapters that follow. As a result of this exercise, citizenship will emerge as a somewhat whimsical and totalitarian—but also deeply utilitarian—legal fiction devoid of moral and ethical *contenu* and ready to be very harsh in punishing the critics of the inequitable in the world it has evolved to perpetuate.

Status

For most people, unlike for Handel and de Lully, citizenship is not chosen and will remain unchanged for life. It is assigned at birth, requiring no intervention whatsoever of the bearer, and whether it ever comes to the bearer's attention at all usually depends on the circumstances. An ordinary American or Dutchman, for example, can live their whole life without thinking about it much. Indeed, while those states style themselves as built by and for their citizens, having the status is precisely invisible and seemingly—but mistakenly—irrelevant to daily life, because citizens are officially "in." Everything changes if you turn to societies where citizens are a minuscule minority, as in ancient Athens or contemporary Qatar.[2] In societies such as these, the vastly outnumbered tyrant citizens surrounded by the deplorable and deportable rightless become acutely aware that their citizenship distinguishes them from this majority of others they happen to be living among. The rightless see this difference very well too— probably much better than the citizens themselves. Such societies base the oppression of the majority by using citizenship (or the lack thereof) as the core justification of the status quo. More subtle variations on the same theme are omnipresent.

Another example, perhaps closer to American hearts, is when you discover that the status you would normally not notice is simply not there. Imagine Juan—he has always thought of himself as an American—who lived in Minnesota, indeed, never left the country, until the moment he discovered he was brought to the United States at the age of three months illegally and had no right to remain, in contrast with his younger sisters born in the country. Similar stories are much more frequent than you would expect (affecting an estimated 2.3 million young people under the age of 24 in 2014 in the United States alone[3]). Examples of similar discoveries from around the world abound. Often-reported stories include Dutch ladies marrying "colonial natives" (*inlanders*) in the East Indies being denied any possibility to return home to Delft or Haarlem since the citizenship status of a married woman had followed that of her husband in the Netherlands since 1898 and colonial natives had no right to move to the Netherlands.[4] Another story concerns the Slovenian "erased": those individuals who failed to notify the authorities that they were taking the citizenship of the newly proclaimed Slovenian state in the wake of the Yugoslav wars, and therefore were left stateless even if born there.[5] In these and countless other examples, which we will be discussing throughout the book, unsuspecting citizens find themselves suddenly plunged into statelessness and illegality. A derailed life is typically the result.

All these examples point in one direction: the formal status of citizenship is of overwhelming importance to everyone's life. Not having it is not the only instance when the status becomes noticeable, however. Indeed, it is only invisible when the one you have is the best available. What if you have citizenship, but its "quality" is dubious? Thinking beyond basic freedoms, such as not caring about who your king or official God is or should be, citizenship sometimes de facto injures lives. De facto it comes with genital mutilation, as in Egypt, where 87 percent of women and girls have been subjected to the procedure;[6] with almost ritual beheadings practiced elsewhere in the Islamic world in punishment for offenses too esoteric for the majority of foreigners to comprehend;[7] or with an absolute prohibition to see the world—think of Turkmenistan, where "exit visas" are virtually never granted.[8] This book will show throughout how much depends on the status of citizenship in theory and also in fact—a reality applicable to all the parts of the world, no matter which citizenship status you hold. Once granted at birth, your citizenship— either Kyrgyz, Modegasque, or Panamanian, it does not matter—determines the treatment, in law and in fact, you will receive *anywhere* in the world. Distributed locally by states, the status of citizenship in each particular case has global implications.

Crucially, although presented as an equally distributed given, citizenship is never and has never been neutral. The status quo it upholds always favors particular interests in a society. Historically, any citizenship status

Citizenship is never and
has never been neutral.

has always played a crucial role in policing strict arbitrary boundaries of exclusion, particularly on the basis of race and sex: although proclaimed equals, women until very recently often neither enjoyed an autonomous citizenship status nor the rights stemming from it, as the colonial Dutch example hinted. Moreover, to claim that non-white colonial subjects were accorded citizenship, either de jure or de facto comparable to that of the "whites" would be an aberration. The neutral status of equals is a powerful tool to instill racist and sexist exclusion. Indeed, doing this has traditionally been one of the core functions of citizenship, as we will see.

It is not necessary to go into the extremes to become aware of the limitations of one's own citizenship. Living the specific nightmare of trying to enter the United Kingdom with a Somali passport is not required. Many high school students in the Netherlands travel around the world upon graduation: the airfares are cheap and seeing many countries in one long trip is a great way to spend a year before going to college—backpack, wash some dishes, wander, compare pot quality, make love—in short, see the world. Once you have the free time and the little money needed to go, all is set for a successful stint of "bumming around," as an English judge once put it.[9] Yet if your citizenship is not Dutch, but say, Moroccan or Kazakhstani, such a trip isn't possible. Needing a separate visa for every stop on the itinerary, there is no point for the kids with such nationalities, however permanent their permit to re-side in the Netherlands may be, to buy a round-the-world ticket: their citizenship quality is below the "minimum" the airlines would presume their customers should have. Moroccans, Kazakhstanis, and countless others will thus remain at home—no matter which country in the world that is—because the citizenship status assigned to them at birth is not "good enough" to travel around the world and, more importantly, to do countless other things too, as we shall discover. The trouble is, a brief glance at the world's citizenship law and practice demonstrates with clarity that the *majority* of citizenships out there are not good enough, negatively affecting the lives of their holders both within and also *outside* the countries of citizenship.

Citizenships assigned at birth without our control remain with us for life in the absolute majority of cases. Beyond travel freedom, they drastically differ in quality: education, prosperity, the mere prospect of living a long and healthy life very much depend on the status you are assigned. Ayelet Shachar has insightfully called this the birthright lottery.[10] The object of the lottery is the status you receive: a ticket to life that can place you in first class, business, or economy light—or indeed, outside the plane. Given the drastic discrepancies and the random assign-ment of citizenship status—you will never be asked which one you want—it is *this status* that lies at citizenship's core. In the basic hierarchy of opportunities, or indeed the chances of physical survival, being an American is radically more privileged than being a Costa Rican, and being a Costa Rican is incomparably better than attachment to Madagascar, as has been measured, for instance, by the Quality of Nationality Index (QNI).[11] The QNI measures comparative quality of all the world's nationalities based on a handful of scientific data points, ranking citizenships based on the freedom of travel, work and residence rights abroad, as well as the human development as reflected in the Human Development Index (HDI), peacefulness, and economic achievements of the issuing country. Differences in the quality of the world's nationalities go much further than whether someone can enter the United States without a visa or work in France without burdensome administrative formalities. Legal statuses matter in the most direct sense. Can you be with the one you love?[12] Can you decide what to believe in or will you be beheaded for apostasy? Will the medical procedure necessary to save your life be available to you? Can you have as many children as you want (or none)? Will your talent let you prosper or will it guarantee that you are impoverished? Crucial aspects of our lives overwhelmingly—and sometimes totally—depend on where we are in the world and which citizenship we hold. The legal status of citizenship formally conferred by the competent authorities in charge of the particular territory is where any story of citizenship is bound to start, to give an accurate account of the concept. That is the basis of the first chapter of this book, which will look at the legal status of citizenship: its assignment, evolution, and prospects for the future.

Rights

Based on the result of the lottery of status distribution, humans who are assigned a legal status obtain rights: indeed, it is the rights accrued via the status that allow distinguishing between the "good" and the "bad" ones. Some statuses (for example, Swiss) can be so advantageous that they nearly guarantee the fortune of a healthy life, good education, freedom of international travel—and also come with options to opt out. Should Switzerland seem too rich or too boring, any Swiss citizen enjoys the right to be admitted, no questions asked, to more than forty other highly developed countries and territories around the world for work and residence, and with strong protections against discrimination on the ground of being "foreign." Other statuses—a bit more, roughly, than half of world citizenships in fact—are a *liability* for each and every holder, compared with what the most highly developed jurisdictions including Switzerland, New Zealand, Ireland, and Luxembourg grant their citizens. Such citizenships undermine lifetime opportunities set glass ceilings, and make dreams unattainable. The popular assumption that the rights citizenships are associated with are comparable, from jurisdiction to jurisdiction, will thus never hold: better statuses grant better rights and more of them; worse statuses create liabilities, sometimes deadly liabilities in fact, instead of granting rights. Dozens of citizenships around the world make living a worthwhile life difficult to impossible. In a world where citizenships play a key role in the spatial ascription of individuals through tying them to the territory of a particular country and where core global inequalities are precisely spatial in nature, as Branko Milanovic has brilliantly demonstrated, citizenships emerge as a key force behind the preservation of the status quo where the poor are poor (the Congolese) and the rich are rich (the Swiss),[13] as we will discuss in further detail. It is crucial to realize that it is citizenship, first of all, as opposed to talent, hard work, and intelligence, that plays the crucial role in our economic well-being, thus emerging as the key tool for the preservation of global inequality.

Economic analysis of global inequality demonstrates that "Our world today is still a world in which the place where we were born or where we live matters enormously, determining perhaps as much as two-thirds of our lifetime income."[14] Only a micropercentage of the world population swapping countries throughout their lifetime escapes the initial ascription of predetermined well-being or ruin. Even more: as a key instrument of the preservation of the global inequality, citizenship wields huge biopower by locking the world's poor in the places where their economic power is nil and life expectancy extremely short. In the crudest example, the chances of reaching the age of five are from twenty-five to fifty times higher among Finnish children than among Congolese children—pick your favorite Congo[15]—but the Finns also have a freedom to reside in dozens of other extremely rich, very high HDI countries,[16] while the Congolese de facto cannot improve their lives via legal migration: their citizenship effectively locks them in. When anyone says "she has her own country and should go back there" about a citizen of any of the world's jurisdictions that offers painful liabilities instead of rights, it is thus not merely unkind, it is also deeply hypocritical, thoughtlessly accepting the mantra of the sovereign equality of states and presenting randomness as justice while regarding dispossession as equality. As we will see throughout the book, the presentation of citizenship in a positive light is virtually always directly connected to the fallacy of assuming that all citizenships are more or less of the same quality and are all connected with more or less usable rights. One of the main goals of this book is to demonstrate that this could not be further from the truth today just as in the past.

Such cozy misrepresentations are enabled through political narratives of self-determination, which are oblivious of the global distribution of economic, political, and cultural power. Numerous popular accounts would insist on political rights as being the only possible starting point for discussion of the essential content of citizenship, granting political rights priority over status. It is sweet to be idealistic, especially if you are a holder of one of the most elite statuses currently available. This is true of the majority of citizenship theorists with the notable exception of Aristotle, a *metic* in the Athenian Republic,[17] tolerated yet forever an alien from Macedon, unlike all North Americans and Western Europeans scribbling textbooks today. Acknowledging one's random privilege is essential to avoid bias against those who are less fortunate and for whom all the political talk is either an annoying irrelevance or an outright pretense, especially when it is invoked as an argument to limit access to a better citizenship—an issue we will turn to in the chapter on the politics of citizenship. In the modern world—as was true 50 or 150 years ago—sanctification of the political rights is one of the pillars supporting the edifice of hypocrisy that makes citizenship, a random status, so appealing and has ensured that it works so effectively, as we will see. Not all of the world's citizenship-conferring jurisdictions today are democracies, not by far. "The Economist Intelligence Unit's Democracy Index" claims that only 4.5 percent of the world's population lives in "Full Democracies." As many as ninety-one countries have "Hybrid" or "Authoritarian" regimes.[18] Democracies are, globally, in retreat.[19] Moreover, all the jurisdictions of the world were sham democracies in a modern sense, in the golden age of nationalist citizenship, when the grand narrative of citizenship as political emancipation was identical to that of today. One should of course be very careful with such decontextualization of democracies. Daniele Archibugi makes this point excellently: "In [Switzerland], voting rights for women (that is, for the majority of the population) were granted only in 1971, much later, for example, than in India. Yet, it would not be correct to conclude that Switzerland was not a democratic system prior to 1971, or that India in 1952 was more democratic than Switzerland."[20]

The core point stands, however: there is infinitely more to citizenship in theory and also in fact than the reproduction of an idea of democratic self-governance. The question arises: Is citizenship dependent on democracy at all then? And if democracies are in retreat, does citizenship follow along? It seems fair to conclude that equating citizenship with democracy has little bearing on its actual functioning in the modern world, outside of a tiny elite group of Western nations, as this book will explain. Overwhelming focus on political participation undermines pretty much all of the core aspects of citizenship as a legal status of attachment to a polity and the crucial rights stemming from this status, in particular the rights of residence and work, as we will discuss in chapter 3. Aristotle was deeply aware of the problem: in his time citizenship existed in the non-democratic societies too, just as it does now—from Qatar to Venezuela and the Central African Republic.[21] The legalistic, Roman conception of citizenship emphasizing the legal status with no relation to how the polity issuing such a status actually governed itself, as analyzed by Michael Oakeshott and Christian Joppke, helps solve this puzzle, while accounting for the citizenship of the majority of the world's states where no democracy is to be found.[22] Indeed, both theory and practice of citizenship considered, points in the direction of a simple fact that fetishization of one particular group of rights only befogs the issue of analyzing citizenship. We will return to this discussion in chapter 5.

Those who notice their citizenship are able to peek beyond the mantras of "sovereign equality," "political participation," and "self-government." The core rights of citizenship include the possibility of living in one's country without the risk of deportation, freedom from constant humiliation and discrimination on the grounds of being "foreign," as well as, crucially, the right to work in the country.

These rights are omnipresent in all the jurisdictions where citizenship exists—from the Greek democracy to the Venezuelan—and should not be exclusive, of course. The fact that Greece allows the Swiss to work in its territory, no questions asked,[23] while providing a Greek bonus on top of the already superb quality of Swiss citizenship, does not necessarily undermine the value of Greek citizenship. Once again: while political rights are important, they are not indispensable to speak of citizenship in practice—an issue Aristotle struggled with as well, as mentioned earlier. It is unquestionable that Sparta, Putin's Russia, Qatar, the Kingdom of the Two Sicilies, and Victorian England, which are equally antidemocratic in that they do not allow the majority of the population to govern itself, nevertheless boast(ed) their own citizenry.

Putting political rights at the forefront, popular as it is, serves some other purpose besides attempting, half-heartedly, to define citizenship. T. H. Marshall, one of the most iconic thinkers in the field, explained the reasons behind this quite vividly as early as just after World War II.[24] Citizenship is about governability and crucially concerns the equal dignity promised to the bearers of the status. In a world where citizenship is an abstraction and equality is its key outcome, individuals' wealth, wit, and capacity to succeed still vary greatly. One person, one vote becomes the core selling point underpinning the mobilization of the populace in support of the status quo as offered by the governing elites—something that the Russian tsar hoped to achieve in 1905: proclaim political rights and by doing so, stop the incipient revolution. Sometimes this works, as T. H. Marshall showed in the example of England; sometimes it does not, as is clear from Russian history.[25] Whether a fiction or reality—usually a blend of the two— citizenship and its rights always come as a package. The third chapter of this book will thus delve into the rights of citizenship, focusing especially on what matters most: in particular residence, work, and settlement rights and their possible exclusivity, evolution, and future trends.

Equality emerges as a bridge between status and rights. Indeed, while being treated without discrimination usually is presented as a right, it also is unquestionably a core element of the status of citizenship as currently understood. Societies can function smoothly, no doubt, with inequality as their foundational ideal. Think of Athenian democracy for instance, under which only a minuscule minority were the bearers of citizenship and the equal worth of human beings was not at all presumed. Indeed, all the day-to-day running of the democratic process was the responsibility of high-ranking slaves owned by the polity.[26] Only the axiomatic presumption of equality based on the equal worth of every person makes contemporary citizenship possible. This can be connected to the articulation of individualism in Christian soteriology—a process splendidly analyzed by Larry Siedentop.[27] The promise of *individual salvation* reversed the classical assumption of justice as a clear apportionment of liberty among nonequals in a "naturally" unequal world. Equality, however empirically problematic, thus emerged as the starting assumption and a powerful normative tool in modern theorizing, which underlies what citizenship, as a status premised on the equal worth of all individuals, means today.

It is individualism that modern citizenship enhances and upholds. The proclamation of the individual's equality, in law, among all citizens is thus a natural device to allow talking about the status of citizenship and the rights connected therewith in the same breath. The ideological baseline of citizenship is the equal worth of every person holding the status—not a family, not a group of people. Of course it is a well-known secret that de facto, unequal citizenship or "semi-citizenship" is thus not only possible but is always the norm in practice, as Elizabeth Cohen has convincingly argued.[28] Yet, from a purely normative perspective, a citizenship of unequals by law as a starting point is not a logical possibility at all.

It is important to realize that the equality we are talking about is not a self-evident or in any sense natural or neutral starting point. It is just a normative position that makes citizenship possible. Sir Isaiah Berlin was right in recalling that "equality is one value among many: the degree to which it is compatible with other ends depends on the concrete situation, and cannot be deduced from general laws of any kind; it is neither more nor less rational than any other ultimate principle; indeed it is difficult to see what is meant by considering it either rational or non-rational."[29]

The idea of equality—first made available according to St. Paul to those who believe—was transposed onto the community of those subjected to a sovereign, first as a prince, then as "the people" following the normative vesting of sovereignty in the latter. That everyone is equal thus came to mean that anyone under the same Prince is equal, and is still based, once the belief is dissected, on a religious dogma. The promise of equality—equal dignity, equal worth—that is so important in the organization of any society, affecting not only our citizenship, but also the basis of morality, is thus not only empirically absent from a world where there are more sovereigns (read: states, peoples) than one. It could ultimately be baseless, if we believe Louis Pojman: "The question is whether the kind of democratic ideals that egalitarians espouse can do without a religious tradition. If it cannot, then egalitarians may be living off the borrowed interest of a religious metaphysic, which (in their eyes) has gone bankrupt."[30]

Baseless should not be read as useless: equality is a crucial normative choice we take. Free from religion or not, egalitarianism is very much alive in the textbooks and official foundational documents every state without any exception produces. Equality is among the key tools to attain legitimacy of power in any democracy. Citizenship both reinforces egalitarianism rhetorically by adopting it as a starting point and necessarily makes it unattainable in practice by confining it within the boundaries of the citizenry. Since the configuration of such boundaries is never neutral—just as the distribution of the actual rights is not—citizenship comes in handy to justify exclusion and to normalize discrimination, not only between but also within societies. This is the reason why the equality claims of any citizenship always fail to convince: precisely by attempting to localize a universal ideal of equality, citizenship is bound to undermine it.

Duties

Any account of citizenship is incomplete without focusing on the duties of citizens, following the old belief that its rights and duties are correlative to each other. Duties consist of a mixed bag of what citizens are expected to perform and the lists are as well known as they are long. "Good citizens" are said to pay taxes, live worthy lives as good members of society, faithfully love their motherland, enlist in the military if required, and be the bearers of the values of their society. Chapter 4 provides a closer inspection of all this. Unlike rights, which may or may not be exclusive to one's status, duties appear to function differently: exclusivity is a requirement here. So, if every resident with an income—or even without any, as in Belarus, where not earning is against the law and taxed at a flat annual rate[31]—is obliged to pay taxes, it is not a duty of citizenship, but rather one of residence: citizenship simply does not apply. The absolute majority of the textbook

Precisely by attempting to localize a universal ideal of equality, citizenship is bound to undermine it.

citizenship duties, quite astonishingly, fail this simple test, but there are usually a couple of exceptions.

With regard to loving the motherland and fighting its wars, for instance, the picture is much more interesting: the rhetoric of duties has consistently been used throughout citizenship's history to infuse phony logic into the deprivation of citizenship rights endured by women, minorities, conscientious objectors, and the indifferent, strengthening the core functions of citizenship— exclusion and complacency. All over the world the picture was the same: women, proclaimed too weak to die for the motherland in any useful way, would thus not receive voting rights or sometimes, de facto, no citizenship rights at all. Citizenship traditionally has always been a masculine status and duties have played the key role in keeping it so.[32] Probably the most interesting aspect of the duties of citizenship story is thus the co-evolution of duties and the contemporary idea of liberty: once the majority of states reinvented themselves away from being hell-bent on destroying minorities and humiliating women, duties started effectively to disappear, as we will discuss in chapter 4. This is not surprising: with duties' core function consisting in the destruction of individuality and the justification of the suspension of the idea of equality— the main underlying principle of citizenship—there is no place for such duties in a context where states start admitting the complexity of the societies they work with. The degree of conflict between the social and the legal reality has been diminishing. Yet, significantly, the historical importance of the duties of citizenship is towering: why should any authority bother to create a citizen in the first place if not to tax him and send him to war? The diminution of duties is thus a story of irony: if duties are not of relevance anymore—a historical pillar underlying the creation of citizenship—what would fill their prominent place on citizenship's façade, saving the concept from further questioning?

Politics

Above all, however, citizenship has always been a political tool wielded by the powers that be, through exclusion, to forge an ephemeral public of their liking: the *demos*. If you need more conscripts, introduce an element of *ius soli* into the otherwise *ius sanguinis* system, as the French did in the late nineteenth century. The French-born children of resident foreigners, themselves born in France, were expected to serve in the military then. As we will see throughout the book, if you dislike a certain ethnic group in your society, pretend that they are not there by defining your citizenry religiously, as the Saudis have done, or ethnically, which will exclude the guys you happen to dislike, as the Latvians and the Estonians have done,[33] deploying the doctrine of state and citizenship continuity and the restoration of sovereignty.[34] If you dislike a political ideology, such as communism, take away communists' passports and citizenship: this was U.S. practice until well into the twentieth century, as brilliantly analyzed by Patrick Weil.[35] The focus has traditionally been on the voting rights of citizens, yet even beyond these rights, the politics of citizenship consists in shaping the population recognized by the state through the claims of political empowerment and "protection," if not "defense" of the body politic from threatening outsiders next door and within. "Who are the *demos*"—a popular issue for political scientists[36]—is thus not a question at all, let alone a relevant question, since the answer is almost too straightforward to be interesting: those whom an authority happened to decide to proclaim citizens and eventually enfranchise some of them in some way in a given context. Ironically, as Daniele Archibugi has perceptively observed, only democracies are interested in the problematization of exclusion through this lens. Indeed, "paradoxically, the all-time enemy of democracy, despotism, has not had to face the problem [of] whom to include: obedience is expected of all individuals."[37] The historical analysis of nation-building worldwide proves this simple point abundantly well. One of the most crucial tools of nation-building is defining its people—citizens or not—from the debates surrounding who is a "German" at the famous 1846 Frankfurt "Germanists Assembly," described so well by Jürgen Habermas,[38] to who is a "Russian" for the first Imperial census,[39] to turning peasants into Frenchmen,[40] to the articulation of all the other "imagined communities"[41] of the world. History strongly cautions against any romanticizations here: citizenship is an effective tool to instill complacency in any society and thus improve its uniformity and governability, no matter who is proclaimed to be in charge—the "people" or Saddam Hussein—as I will demonstrate throughout the book. Democracies, like totalitarian regimes, have been equally effective on this count, ensuring citizenship's universalism in the contemporary world.

Once the law is clear, good citizens—the main product and the main evil of citizenship at work—will report their neighbors who are "Jews" sullying "Aryan maidens," in the words of Hitler's *Mein Kampf*, or who are "Aryans" but dating "Jewish" women—both perversions against the honor of the nation policed exclusively by well-meaning neighbors, family members, and friends. As Patricia Szobar and colleagues have shown: "The majority of race-defilement cases were initiated by a denunciation rather than through the Gestapo's own investigative efforts."[42] Creating categories in law brings these to life and social conventions, practices, and prejudices follow. Different U.S. states had different approaches, for instance, to defining who was a "negro"; race of a person thus changes by moving from one state to another. A "negro" in Louisiana was someone with more than $\frac{1}{32}$ of African American blood, while in Oregon—more than $\frac{1}{4}$. Utah law spoke of "mulattoes," "quadroons," and "octoroons."[43] That in each case who is a "negro," who is an "octoroon," and who is "white" was supposed to be treated by the locals as "objective reality"[44] is as good an example of how the law and political discourse shapes society as American racial profiling today: "Hispanics" is a well-understood category in the United States, which does not exist elsewhere in the world—outside of the Americas that is—and is bound to leave your Basque and Catalan friends puzzled. Purely legal truths thus spill into the imaginary real life and affect and inform social reality. Legal "world-making" in Pierre Bourdieu's terminology,[45] or, similarly, the production of "legal truths" in the words of Jack Balkin,[46] probably belongs to one of the most fascinating aspects of the practical functioning of the law. Indeed, setting ideas in law that make and remake our world and citizenship—both abstract and disconnected in the majority of cases from personal choices and desires, is one of the most telling examples of such "world-making." In the "state of nature" there are, obviously, no citizens.

The politics of citizenship is thus not so much how and when citizens use political rights to elect representatives, but more to the point, why such rights are reserved for citizens and who the citizens actually are at any given moment as their body fluctuates constantly in every polity. It is not who votes—it is who is a citizen. The politics of citizenship is the politics of access to the status and rights of citizenship. Naturalizations, denaturalizations, expatriations, playing with the intergenerational transfer of citizenship rules, the enfranchisement and disenfranchisement of different classes of citizens abroad and inside a country, the recourse to the rhetoric of duties to exclude huge vulnerable populations—these are just some ingredients of the politics of citizenship, as chapter 5 of this book shows.

Identity: A Disclaimer

Before we turn to examining the status, rights, duties, and politics of citizenship in detail, a small disclaimer about identity is in order. The static totalitarianism of "good citizenship" is best reflected in the identitarian element of the status, which some would even regard as part of the very definition of the concept. Certainly, citizenship is about belonging to a big family of friends, sticking together in this hostile world! Identity goes to the core of the idea of the self, yet it is doubly irrelevant in the world of citizenship. First, citizenship is about a status assigned by law, which is not chosen, since only about 2 percent of the world's population would actually change their citizenship throughout their lifetime, 98 percent thus relying on whatever legal status they were assigned at birth. The story of Maria Toet documented by Betty de Hart is a good illustration of how identity works: Maria married a Polish man in 1940 and thereby lost her Dutch citizenship. When the marriage collapsed—the man was an abusive alcoholic—and Poland slid into a new, Soviet-style dictatorship following Marshall Piłsudski and the occupation— the Dutch state absolutely refused to give her a residency permit. Having overstayed her visa and been a fugitive from Dutch law enforcement, and having escaped an abusive husband at home, Maria presumably had sufficient Dutch identity, but it is not identity that makes citizenship. Certainly, identity cannot defeat the sexist core of the notion. The law was only changed to enable Dutch women to retain their citizenship upon marriage to a foreigner in 1985—effectively the first year women could be regarded as "real" citizens in the Netherlands.[47]

Identity does not work the other way around either. Imagine you are ashamed of your country and believe it to be an aberration of justice: take Apartheid South Africa, for instance. Whatever you may feel and no matter how much you may refuse to share the ideals the country stands for, this does not affect your citizenship at all. A second example, corresponding to the racist grain in citizenship, might include the majority population rejecting your identity. As a Jewish convert to Christianity, Hernando de Talavera was so Spanish and such a fervent Catholic that he rose to become archbishop of Granada and the confessor of Queen Isabel herself. This did not prevent him from dying at the hands of the Inquisition, who deeply distrusted "new Christians," as Antonio Feros reports.[48] "You speak German well for a Turk" is something we hear every day in the streets of Hamburg and Berlin, where it is usually addressed to a third-generation German. The examples of identity failing to help because it contradicts the law and the law failing to help in the face of overwhelming prejudice both argue for strong reservations about including identity as a part of the definition of citizenship. To try to define "citizenship" through any kind of cultural-linguistic affinity to a nation is thus entirely beside the point: whatever you think your identity is, citizenship can—and often will—be denied by law. The reverse is equally true: anyone holding a citizenship status who does not boast the expected identity remains a citizen no matter what—be it an Uruguayan who was born and grew up in the United States; a hippie fleeing the draft; or a dual German-Israeli citizen pulling out a German passport at a U.S. border-crossing point, however many reservations she would have against the status provided by that particular state and however little association she has with Germany (an Israeli passport does not give visa-free travel to America, so the choice here is quite obvious, whether one speaks German and knows the Chancellor's name, or not). To connect citizenship with identity is thus nothing but intellectual laziness. Identity only matters when the

To connect citizenship with identity is thus nothing but intellectual laziness.

people on the street and the powers that be want to *exclude* you from equality and other rights no matter what status you may think you have. However, a particular identity in itself is of course not required—it is indeed irrelevant—in order to hold the status and possibly enjoy the rights of citizenship, where such rights are provided at all.

Constant Evolution

Crucially, citizenship status, rights, duties, and politics—all the elements of citizenship outlined previously—are in a state of constant dynamic co-evolution, which affects their weight and importance in the context of citizens' lives and state governance. The starting point of every citizenship debate—the Aristotelian account—is so intellectually removed from us that any allusion to it must indispensably be made with a grain of salt. Predating individualism, in Aristotle's society each citizen stood for a tightly knit clan cemented by a home religion that put the family and its ancestors at the center.[49] Moreover, rather than holding equality as its main value, inequality, perceived of as absolutely natural, was the ideal of justice.[50] We are a long way from that approach to the world, as both core ideals have flipped: men now stand for themselves and have individual equal moral worth (and women now finally count, too): that is what citizenship today is said to promote. Besides, from regarding ordinary work as unfit for a citizen in the anti-just society of Aristotle (from our perspective at least), work is now, alongside residence, among the core rights of citizens. Let us therefore be scrupulously careful when mentioning Aristotle in relation to citizenship.

The core ideas of citizenship have changed just as drastically over the last 100 years, however: one does not need to travel to ancient Athens. The general line of development, as we shall see throughout this book, is to extend the status of citizenship increasingly to those who are part of the society in question but are excluded and, similarly, to extend the rights that used to be uniquely citizenship rights to those who do not hold the status. In the same vein, there are increasingly fewer citizens without rights: women now vote, the remaining communists can have passports, and the speakers of minority languages generally are not harassed into forgetting their culture under the banner of good citizenship.[51] Increasingly many citizenships can be cumulated: the previously implicit exclusivity of the status is waning. As the rights and the scope of their application expand, so does the territory of their application. Increasingly, many countries grant foreign citizens full equality and access to crucial citizenship rights in their own territories—either reciprocally, such as in the European Union, MERCOSUR, the Gulf Cooperation Council, the Eurasian Economic Union, or unilaterally. The mantra "one *demos*—one state—one territory of rights" no longer holds in the world, with the exception of a handful of particularly old-fashioned countries, such as Canada and Madagascar, as we will see in chapter 3. A Norwegian can settle, work, and stay as long as he pleases in the forty-one richest and highest developed countries and territories around the globe without being discriminated against on the grounds of being precisely that—a Norwegian. For a citizen of Cape Verde the figure is fourteen; for the United Arab Emirates (UAE) it is six; for Belarus, five. Exceptions can also be observed. Both Pakistanis and the Chinese belong to just under half of the world's nationalities not welcome to settle anywhere outside their own state, as discussed in detail in chapter 3 and illustrated by figure 6.

Some foundational and historical pillars of citizenship are slowly crumbling, depriving citizenship of its core function and purpose. Indeed, all the key current citizenship trends render exclusion and the randomness of assignment of rights and privileges extremely difficult to justify. Citizenship's sexism, its racism, and its abuse of individuality through appeals to the ideals of good citizenship and especially the duty to be "good" are in retreat, making contemporary citizenship differ even more from what it was only fifty years ago. Yet all the advances of recent evolution could not erase the gradations in the levels of enjoyment of rights, of course: equal citizenship is as mythical today as it ever was before, notwithstanding all the fundamental changes that make it more equal, more tolerant, and less totalitarian.

A critical *parcour* through citizenship via the status, rights, duties, and politics as key elements is bound to produce a picture of citizenship that is very far from the optimistically glossy popular one, thus exposing the poisonous ideology underpinning the concept. Citizenship is an official celebration of equality, yet its main function is random exclusion. Citizenship is an official trope for political empowerment, yet the natural effect of its successful operation is complacency. Citizenship is about celebrating an identity, yet identity is not a necessary element of the citizenship package as we have seen. Moreover, citizenship's recent evolution points toward discrediting the "good citizen" mythology. Citizenship is about rights in the sovereign territory, yet current trends in rights and the evolution of territoriality make sustaining this correlation truly untenable for numerous nations around the world.

STATUS

Citizenship is foremost a legal status of belonging. If you are considered by the U.S. authorities to be Tanzanian but think of yourself as an American, whatever your reasons might be for that, you will be sent back to Tanzania with a smile immediately after touchdown at JFK airport. In fact, you will most likely not even be able to board the plane in Tanzania in the first place. If, on the other hand, the U.S. authorities consider you to be an American, you will face a demand to pay U.S. taxes even if you have never lived in the country, no matter how much outrage this causes you, unless you decide to renounce the status, just as the extravagant UK Prime Minister Boris de Pfeffel Johnson did, outraged by a capital gains tax bill from the Internal Revenue Service of a country he had not lived in since the age of five. Johnson joined a fast-growing group of former Americans making U.S. citizenship one of the most desired but also one of the most renounced citizenships in the world.[1] A crucial, sometimes misunderstood lesson emerges: the status of citizenship cannot be self-ascribed, as its conferral is monopolized by the state authorities around the world. Citizenship thus inhabits a legal reality, which does not necessarily overlap with the social one, although the law would of course claim otherwise. Do not be misled: citizenship's very raison d'être is to guarantee and perpetuate the cleavage between the two.

Abstract and Totalitarian

Moreover, citizenship is an abstract status. The fact that someone is a Norwegian or a Pakistani does not have anything to do with the character, talents, education, or aspirations of the person in question. Loving Pakistan or Norway is officially expected and proclaimed a necessity by law, but failing to do so will not deprive you of your citizenship. Otherwise, depending on the decision of the competent authorities, anyone can be born a Norwegian, just as anyone can be born a Pakistani, in all cases regardless of what they themselves think of the country. Abstract and essentially impersonal, citizenship is totalitarian in nature: it does not emerge in "dialogue" and is much less flexible than many would like to think. Citizenship is not a status based on one's wishes or choice. It has nothing at all to do with free association. It is a binding claim of loyalty and unconditional legal subjugation independent of one's wishes or preferences, which cannot be rebutted or refused. Furthermore, it is even impossible to renounce, as we shall see, unless you have acquired an alternative one, if at all. So better start loving your country and your citizenship, which is precisely what patriots do, forging internal coherence in Benedict Anderson's "imagined communities,"[2] necessarily random in nature. Citizenship is a crucial and necessary stepping-stone on the road to nationalism.

The abstract status disconnected from the individuality of the bearer nevertheless assigns the bearer a clear value both internally and externally, a value entirely disconnected from any other characteristic besides the citizenship status itself. A Norwegian travels the world not noticing international borders and enjoys remarkable benefits of excellent education, healthcare, and social support in one of the richest and most equitable countries in the world. This is as opposed to a Pakistani, who is de facto not welcome anywhere without strict pre-travel vetting and who will live a much shorter life, infinitely poorer in opportunities for self-fulfillment. Worse still, a Pakistani will live her life without any options to settle abroad legally without hassle, thus not much trusted or loved by other states, as opposed to the adored Norwegian, who is able

Citizenship is a crucial and necessary stepping-stone on the road to nationalism.

to settle and work without any formalities in forty-one of the richest states and territories around the world as discussed earlier. Not that Norwegians are "better" than Pakistanis, of course—the contrary may be the case, depending on what you value in a person. Norwegian citizenship, however, is infinitely better without any doubt. Since the status is as abstract within as it is between states, Anders Behring Breivik, who massacred seventy-seven people in Norway in July 2011 out of hate and racist beliefs,[3] enjoys as many protections and entitlements as a citizen of Norway as any other Norwegian does, and will also benefit as much—albeit from his jail cell. He currently studies political science in solitary confinement—for free of course—as a part-time student of the University of Oslo. Compare him with Malala Yousafzai, the youngest Nobel Prize winner, who was shot in Pakistan for the belief that girls should be entitled to education.[4] She is no better or worse a Pakistani in the eyes of her domestic law as any other citizen of that country: her life is as much affected by the citizenship status she holds as is the life of her attacker.

Citizenship is a formal abstract status of equals within the boundaries of the law of the authority conferring it. Thus equality is the first and most important fundamental assumption underlying the status. The citizens' many distinct personal traits, talents, and bank account balances notwithstanding, they benefit from it in the same, equal way, we are told. Equality is generally applied to all the citizens in a society holding the status, not just to a minority. All those lacking the status are excluded. Citizenship is thus endowed with strictly bounded generality.

Another assumption behind the abstract status is that we cannot compare the holders of different citizenships. A Pakistani, "good" or "bad," is thus presumed to be infinitely different from an equally abstract Norwegian. Moreover, it is also presumed that this difference is somewhat natural and therefore does not cause ethical or moral problems in the face of the differences in the rights and life prospects of those assigned by the chance of birth to different states. The world of citizenship is thus presented to us as a happy one: everyone—almost everyone—in the world is a holder of a citizenship status ascribing that person to an authority, and this ascription guarantees equal enjoyment of rights and equal subjection to obligations within the realm of that authority's jurisdiction. To quote from Richard Bellamy's popular book, citizenship is about "influencing government policy according to reasonably fair rules and on a more or less equal basis with others."[5] Citizenship is presented as a rational, logical, and positive political status of equals—a status that is therefore ultimately just: an achievement of modernity, bringing with it dignity, equality, and rights, but also responsibilities.

What is often forgotten in the context of retelling such triumphant stories of justice is that behind the charges of hypocrisy the abstract coin of citizenship has another, uglier, side. Precisely because there is no correlation between individual persons' character and abilities and the citizenship assigned to them, the abstractness of citizenship turns the status into a random punishment for the significant proportion of the world's population who get a terrible deal through association with substandard statuses, like the Pakistani one, which effectively obstruct, rather than foster the living of safe, dignified, and fulfilling lives. Indeed, while abstractness is essentially the core added value—at least in theory—of forging the idea of citizenship in the first place, it would only truly work in a world where the authorities issuing the status guarantee at least roughly comparable standards of self-fulfillment and personal empowerment. In such a world it would not matter which status you hold. In a world where there are Pakistanis and Norwegians, however—as opposed to only Norwegians and, say, Danes—the story of equal dignity barely holds. Of course, a homicidal Norwegian is still a Norwegian with all a Norwegian's rights. But the same applies to our Pakistani: however great, she will still remain precisely that, a Pakistani, along with all the unfortunate liabilities of a citizenship of that country.

Global Inequality Tool

The assumption of the incomparability of different citizenships coupled with the belief in their inherent worth and dignity allows the status of citizenship to play one of its core functions in the modern world. This function consists in the justification and perpetuation of global inequality. Indeed, when key inequalities used to be concentrated *within* as opposed to *between* states, citizenship as a status of equals—politically at least—could mitigate inequalities, at least to some extent. After inequalities moved to rest *between* states, however, as Branko Milanovic has demonstrated, all this changed.[6] It takes erecting migration walls between societies to turn state citizenship into an instrument of oppression and subjugation, which cements—and also glorifies in the eyes of the believers in the dignity of citizenship—the overwhelming gap between Norway and Pakistan. Joseph Carens, the leading scholar of the moral foundations of citizenship, is closer to the truth than the majority of the textbooks used in citizenship education around the world: citizenship is but a "modern equivalent of feudal privilege."[7] Erecting impenetrable walls shutting out the citizens of the neediest and most poorly governed nations explains why the rubber boats cross the Mediterranean in one direction only.

The crucial role of spatial as opposed to class inequalities has been abundantly proven by economists and demonstrates beyond any reasonable doubt that it is the place on the globe where your life is lived as opposed to your particular background that is fundamental for your economic situation—no matter your profession—and all the related factors, such as education and life expectancy. Although this is a proven fact, it is not at all internalized, in particular not in the prosperous West. Given that an annual income of USD 80,000 already places you among the top 1 percent by income in the world, it is clear that the majority of the Occupy Wall Street protestors, for instance, belonged if not to the top 1 percent they were purportedly rallying against, then to the world's super-elite, at a minimum. They themselves failed to realize this, of course, since class inequality, although negligible in the contemporary world compared with the humongous scale of the spatial one, still occupies the leading place on the agenda in contemporary politics. This is the working of citizenship that assigns everyone in the world randomly to "their place": geographically, but also, significantly, economically and biologically, by putting a cap on incomes and life expectancy.[8] Citizenship quality and global wealth distribution correlate very neatly with each other as is illustrated by Benjamin Hennig's research in figure 1: the map of the world is rescaled based on the GDP and the darker regions correlate to higher citizenship quality using the Quality of Nationality Index methodology. A radically different map of the world is produced by rescaling it depending on

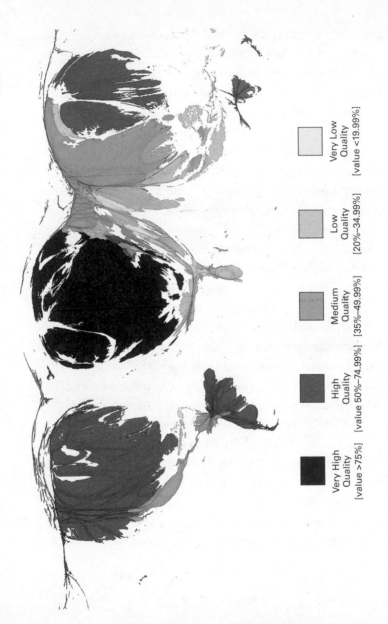

Figure 1 Citizenship quality and wealth

Source: B. D. Hennig, "In Focus: The Quality of Nationality," *Political Insight* 20 (2018): 9.

Very High
Quality
[value >75%]

High
Quality
[value 50%–74.99%]

Medium
Quality
[35%–49.99%]

Low
Quality
[20%–34.99%]

Very Low
Quality
[value <19.99%]

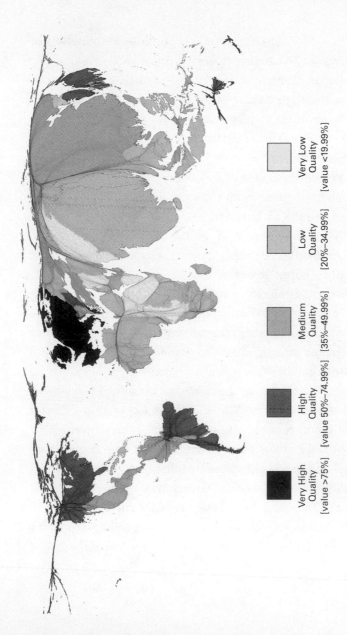

Figure 2 Citizenship quality and population
Source: B. D. Hennig, "In Focus: The Quality of Nationality," *Political Insight* 20 (2018): 9.

Very High
Quality
[value >75%]

High
Quality
[value 50%–74.99%]

Medium
Quality
[35%–49.99%]

Low
Quality
[20%–34.99%]

Very Low
Quality
[value <19.99%]

the population, as in figure 2. It becomes absolutely clear that while the absolute majority of the most economically developed countries offer their people elite super citizenships, the biggest share of the population of the world are the losers of the lottery and live with substandard citizenship statuses. This is the most important vector of global inequality reinforced by democracies and autocracies alike.

Where the levels of development in the OECD and elsewhere in the world are so radically different, it will take more than a hundred years—at least for China and at the current levels of global economic growth—to bridge the divide. In this context, the most obvious, but usually ignored aspect of development is migration. Milanovic is absolutely justified in claiming that the Gulf states are crucially important actors in the promotion of global development: all the workers they invite—however mistreated and rightless they emerge in the eyes of the Western public—are given a chance of improving their economic situation in the most radical way.[9] This is an option that the United States and the EU certainly do not offer, having erected visa walls precisely to keep the holders of the world's worst citizenships at bay, however talented and promising these people may be. In fact, while providing nothing like the Gulf States' opportunities, the United States and the EU even criticize the Qatar and the UAE's openness to labor migration as a failure to guarantee "equality" and "dignity"—arch-hypocrisy of the walled communities dictating to the world outside their walls who should be let in and under which conditions.

Citizenship is thus a violent tool of inequitable distribution of the basic life chances around the globe. The violence of this reality is attested to by the loss of life among those who do not buy the status quo: more than fifteen thousand dead in the Mediterranean according to the Office of the United Nations High Commissioner for Refugees (UNHCR) and over fifteen hundred dead in the Arizona desert between 2012 and 2017 alone. Sixteen thousand five hundred people dying while trying to cross an inequitably preassigned border of opportunity is a minuscule number compared with the population of all the countries whose citizenship is a liability, which is billions and counting. Citizenship emerges in a radically different light from *within* the bounded bastions of the richest countries and from the other parts of the world. This radical discrepancy only increases as the richest countries open up to each other and create a cosmopolitan and open image of the world for those who hold their citizenships. James Tully is right in his analysis of the triumphant march of modern citizenship around the world: "The globalization of modern citizenship has not tended to democracy, equality, independence and peace, as its justificatory theories proclaim, but to informal imperialism, inequality, dependence and war. This tendency is intrinsic to the modern mode of citizenship as a whole."[10]

The picture Tully painted is unquestionably true to life today. What prevents this reality from spoiling the rosy image of citizenship? There are at least four fictions at play here, all of them most conveniently embraced to such an extent that one does not usually think at all about the biases underpinning each of them. The first is basic nationalism: "our" society of citizens is more just and composed of better people as opposed to "theirs"—be it Canadians, Russians, or Afghanis. This makes all of us special and intimately connected to each other. Of course we are worthy of more rights, protections, and attention than any foreigner.

Every morning—and especially on June 20, which is Flag Day—sleepy Argentinian children recite the pledge to the flag. They are asked

> to promise to produce your most sincere and
> respectful homage, to love it and form it with
> immense love, from the dawn of the life a fervent
> and indelible cult in your hearts; preparing
> yourselves from the school to practice to its time,
> with all purity and honesty, the noble virtues
> inherent in citizenship, studying with determination
> the history of our country and that of its big
> benefactors in order to continue its luminous traces
> and to end also of honoring the Flag and of which
> there should never get depressed in your souls the
> delicate and generous love feeling to the Fatherland.

Of course every one of more than two hundred "Fatherlands" around the globe uses similar devices, while no concrete examples of "noble virtues inherent in citizenship" are in sight outside of the cocoon of any given state. From the cradle we are trained to think that the foreigner does not have a claim to rights no matter what her culture, or where she is—a continent away, or in the same apartment block with us since the moment of her birth. The second assumption, which flows from the first, and already mentioned, is that all the citizenships are equally dignifying and dignified, just as all the states around the world are under contemporary international law. Never mind that you are born a Pakistani: poorer chances in a life lived in a cage that the citizenship as a liability guarantees is equal to what an elite and profoundly empowering status such as Norwegian citizenship that is actually centered on rights will bring, on this commonplace legalistic account. Third, there is a tacit presumption that citizens live at "home": a Liechtensteiner in the sixty-two square miles of national territory and an Australian in the huge vastness of the southern continent. In other words, we are presented with a picture where equal and worthy states are inhabited by their citizens, and never mind any others. The fourth, and probably the most misleading of the four assumptions, is that citizenship is indispensable for political "self-determination" and defending it from those who are proclaimed foreign is a value in itself helping each society to be free. We will discuss the hypocrisy of this powerful narrative in chapter 5.

All four assumptions described are indispensable to eagerly embrace the world of modern citizenship and the edifice of modern politics, effectively closing our eyes to the core functions of this status today and in the past. Here then is the paradox: while these assumptions are, unsurprisingly, quite unhelpful from the perspective of any lay person, these same assumptions are staunchly supported by most lawyers and political scientists as necessary and, ultimately, just. Their absurdity is entirely ignored, then, in the face of their perceived useful effects, their essential and untenable abstractness almost ritually forgotten.

There is a reason why the majority of philosophers and political scientists forget the obvious contradictions. Citizenship is designed to function in the context of *one* country. Key theorists including T. H. Marshall, John Rawls, and Ronald Dworkin thus almost naturally appear to assume that every collective exists in a vacuum. Such a perspective justifies closing one's eyes at virtually *all* the essential features of citizenship as a legal-political phenomenon, which play out, as this book demonstrates, precisely outside the one-nation context. Your citizenship is a passport to the whole world that will boost your chances to succeed in whatever you do or bring you down *anywhere*, also outside the boundaries of the authority that conferred it. Once one realizes that vacuum has never been an accurate description of the "outside" and that surrounding each citizenship with such "terra incognita," which has never been and is no longer useful, the intellectual complacency of the dominant whitewashing of the status quo in citizenship writing can no more be upheld as tenable. The most respected mainstream theorists are not concerned with what is outside, thereby ignoring the core aspects of the essence of citizenship. Treating the bounded community of citizens as an unquestionable given, the mainstream theory is not only unrealistic, but also almost impossibly dull, since it emerges as squarely nationalist, as Linda Bosniak, among numerous others, has rightly diagnosed.[11] The core question, which the mainstream theorists tend to ask is thus "what are the justifications for inclusion?" This question obviously misses the key point, endorsing the harms produced by citizenship without questioning them, by accepting that the citizen/non-citizen distinction does not need a justification. Making the inequitable status quo seem natural, no questions asked, is the triumph of the morality and dignity of citizenship.

Given that the abstract nature of the status of equals is the main point of citizenship, non-citizens are not entitled to the same treatment as citizens in an ideal citizenship world. Moreover, the reasons behind the distribution of the status do not enter the picture at all: they are absolutely irrelevant when possible inequalities are discussed.

Making the inequitable
status quo seem natural,
no questions asked,
is the triumph of the
morality and dignity
of citizenship.

While the national border has long ceased its function as the frontier between the Empire—civilization—and the barbarians, the duality, which we find in the Roman imagination, equating the confines of the state with civilization is still the norm presumed every day—even if not admitted openly. "He is not a citizen" is always a generally accepted and fully sufficient explanation to justify discounting or even discarding someone's dignity. The world of citizenship is thus a vehicle for assaulting the dignity of those inside and outside any country: exclusion from the status is the only step required to make this seem logical.

In the 2015 parliamentary elections in Estonia, the lowest turnout was recorded in Ida-Viru county, of which Narva is the biggest city. During the acceptance speech the newly elected prime minister said: "Nüüdsest on meil vaja teha keerulisi otsuseid, raskeid valikuid ja leida vastused suurtele väljakutsetele." Just like you, presumably, the citizens of Narva could not quite follow. Only 3.86 percent of the population of the city belongs to "ethnic Estonians" according to the government of the divided post-Soviet microstate, and the others, although sometimes in Estonia for many generations, belong to the frowned-upon "Russian-speaking" minority, their language prohibited in a political context and their citizenship not immediately secure.[12] This example teaches us that in the eyes of the authorities, citizens do not all live "at home" or speak the right language, whatever 96.15 percent of a city's population might think of their home town of Narva and of the Russian language they sing lullabies in. The mayor, whom 46 percent of the city's population who actually have the right papers elected, was recently fined by the state authorities for using a "foreign language" in his official role— the language of more than 96 percent of his constituency.[13]

Similar stories come from neighboring Latvia, where the mayor of Riga—largely a Russian-speaking city in a country keen on punishing any deviations from the recently installed "official language"—was fined for using Russian on Facebook to communicate with the residents of his city who do not know the "official language."[14] Legal truth, while *ab initio* presumed to be successful in shaping the world, never overlaps entirely with social reality. The scale of the discrepancy between the two varies, and while Narva obviously is an extreme example, it is a telling one. Other extreme examples are numerous. The idea that citizens remain overwhelmingly in their country of citizenship and fully embrace the proclaimed culture only really verges on truth in the case of the most atrocious totalitarian states: North Koreans indeed live in North Korea and Turkmen in Turkmenistan. These citizenships are so oppressive—they make it difficult to escape the beloved motherland, thus effectively switching off the rest of the world for the unfortunate holders of these statuses, bringing them much closer than other nations—if that is a consolation—to the Marshallean ideal. Our planet outside the national border walls is thereby turned into a myth, its content blurred and unsure. In other places, however, the correlation by definition cannot hold for all: free people settle where they please, no matter what the local law dictates.

Indeed, this is probably the best thing about immigration law: it cannot switch off human agency, no matter how many walls are built—and how fancy the designs.[15] The foundational assumption behind it—however useful the regulation of borders might be in practice and however prevalent the teaching of myopic ideologies that refuse to recognize a world beyond the border—is bound to remain profoundly questionable. This is because an introspection akin to "it is our society, we fenced off this land" lacks any truly convincing global justifications. Joseph Carens is absolutely right on this count: "No moral argument will seem acceptable to us, if it directly challenges the assumption of the equal moral worth of all individuals."[16] This is precisely why any border presents such a conundrum of ethical difficulties: it is impossible to justify its intrinsic value. Even when praised by a leader, supporting arguments for a wall are unlikely to convince those whose dignity it denies and whose lives it obstructs. People locked in will jump the wall, even at risk of being killed. People locked out will jump the wall too, of course, just to use the German Democratic Republic and the United States as examples of such breached barriers. Crucial here is the fact that in any state in the world there will be no absolute correlation between the population—call it a society—on the one hand, and the body of citizenry on the other. This is not only true because of the deep inequalities between states and the differences in the quality of their citizenships. Diversity also matters: a different society, even if not necessarily better or worse than your own, is attractive precisely due to the fact that it is not the same. Curiosity and the sense of exploration are as much a part of human nature as is the desire to enslave others, while glorifying those like yourself, to dehumanize, and to build walls. Citizenship epitomizes a natural conflict.

The status of citizenship produces the body of citizens—an abstract ephemeral society, which does not overlap with one including all the inhabitants of any place or those sensing affinity to it—and by definition excludes all the "foreigners"—those who do not hold this abstract legal status. In this sense, citizenship is a parallel reality compared with the one observable in the streets: not each and every one of your neighbors is a citizen. The legal reality behind the distribution of the citizenship status could draw inspiration from the social reality of the society on the ground, but it does not have to, per se. In fact, the majority of citizens can also be abroad—as is the case of Cape Verde or the Cook Islands.[17] And of course, citizens can be a very small minority: Qatar and the United Arab Emirates are cases in point, where citizens make up 12 percent and 11.32 percent of the population,[18] respectively. Whether in the minority or in the majority, no non-citizen is cherished as equal to a citizen in the eyes of the law. This is the "natural" reality throughout the world, which citizenship has been designed to install and defend at the expense of those humiliated by it.

This brief overview of the assumptions underlying citizenship brings us to the two core functions of citizenship. Citizenship consists in drawing a line of exclusion through a society, thus *forging a new collective* of those who are declared to be citizens, proclaiming *them* the true holders of identity, rights, and protections, and entitled to equality, dignity, and freedom, and *protecting this abstract collective* from the impurities of foreignness. The interplay between these two interrelated functions gave citizenship one of its best definitions to date: "an instrument and an object of closure," coined by Rogers Brubaker several decades ago.[19] The status of citizenship thus constitutes and excludes at the same time. In doing this, it endows each state with two borders: the immigration border and the citizenship border. States vary in which of the two they make impenetrable for those whom they proclaim as outsiders. It is very easy to settle in Dubai, but acquiring citizenship is almost impossible. The contrary is true of the United States: once you settle there legally—which is relatively difficult—naturalization is usually not a problem at all.

Randomness versus Choice

The essential story behind the status of citizenship is that the assignment of this status is not based on choice and is both random and actively rationalized by commentators and citizens alike. Such rationalizations are of course more convincing for the holders of elite citizenships of the most developed countries around the world than for the remaining 82 percent—more than four-fifths—of the world's population.[20] With so much at stake from life-long economic prosperity to education and life expectancy, citizenship plays an essential role in everyone's life. In this context, the logic underlying the distribution of the citizenship status should be particularly clear and convincing. The contrary is what we have in practice. The distribution of life chances around the globe is not reliant on any factors at all that would connect to the traits of the individual holders of the status received—besides the color of the skin in the diminishing number of openly racist countries. Outside of those racist countries the distribution is thus entirely random from the individual citizen's point of view. This is a huge problem, given how radically different the quality of different citizenships is. As an instrument of the preservation of spatial inequality in the world disconnected from any acceptable substantive justification, citizenship is thus an aberration of justice.

While countless ways of acquiring a legal status are available, the variation, once we abstract ourselves from the legal nitty-gritty, is not that huge. Ultimately, two core approaches or, to be more precise, a mixture between the two, are responsible for the distribution of the absolute majority of citizenships around the world. Both have ancient roots reaching back to pre-citizenship times. They are *ius sanguinis*—the blood rule attachment to the authority claiming your parents (or at least one of them)— and *ius soli*—the attachment of the status to the authority that happens to claim your place of birth: allegiance to those governing the territory. While sometimes presented as being in competition with each other, both traditionally have been of critical importance to the determination of the legal statuses people held: all the countries in the world with the sole exception of the Vatican City State have the elements of both on their books.

Ius sanguinis is as ancient as it is easy to explain: a son of a slave is a slave, a daughter of a nobleman is noble, and a son of a Belgian is Belgian. *Ius soli* is trickier, as it implies territoriality, not only a collective under someone's authority. Accordingly, anyone born in the realm claimed by the English king used to be English, everyone born in the United States is still American. While aristocratic titles, just like bonded states of slaves and serfs, are usually inherited by *ius sanguinis* and with numerous exceptions (such as paternal line, firstborn, and many others)—allegiance to a king would frequently be territorial: once born on his land, you owed him taxes, love, and if he says it is necessary, your life—a random offer you couldn't refuse. As time went on, *ius soli* and *ius sanguinis* would succeed each other in turn as the most popular ways to assign the status.

Even when the core status assignment is *ius sanguinis*-based, territory usually lurks conspicuously near. Aristotelian Athens is a great example: citizens were an extreme minority of free men who inherited the status through the paternal line, but all officially traced their origins to the mythical act of indigenous birth from the Earth of Athens itself, as Stuart Elden, among others, wonderfully described. The myth of autochthonous birth, although already recognized by Plato in the *Republic* as a "noble lie," was extremely popular and had a vital, if xenophobic, function, which was to teach Athenians the worth of others: "not foreigners, nor are these their sons settlers in this land, descended from strangers who came to our country from abroad. These men were autochthonous, sprung from the land itself, living and dwelling in their true fatherland," Aspasia suggests in Socrates' retelling.[21] Obvious connection to the place in the legend notwithstanding, it was the status of the father that determined the status of the son: "citizenship" was a privilege for a small male minority.

Applying contemporary approaches to the ancient societies of Greece and Rome is inconvenient of course and also potentially misleading. This is not only because their "citizenships" lacked, through slaveholding and the exclusions of women, the core elements of generality and equality that are now cherished as fundamentally important parts of the notion. Crucially, the moral intuitions of these societies—their ethical foundations—were radically different from ours. They prized the idea of inequality greatly, as one of the main values underlying human relations in reflecting the supposedly natural order of things. It was uncontested at that time that humans belonged to naturally emerging groups, incomparable to each other, making individuality—indispensable for any general egalitarian thinking—impossible. Contemporary citizenship, to the contrary, like pretty much every key precept of contemporary law, is markedly individualistic. As Larry Siedentop has persuasively argued, this individualism is traceable to the evolution of canon law from the early Middle Ages on, reflecting in law the belief in salvation as an *individual* rather than a clan or tribal matter. The equality of souls in the eyes of God came to be translated into the reversal of the belief in natural inequality, deeply held in antiquity.[22]

Newly emerged individualism enabled the idea of equality before the law, eventually leading to the idea of a political community. Ultimately faith and submission amounted to key elements of it, with both emerging as fundamental stepping-stones of personhood in the law. Belonging to the Christian faith allowing for individual salvation and, following similar logic, to the body politic through allegiance to your monarch, underpinned a radical change in the earlier common vision of the individual's place in the world. Once again: this reversal is integral to our contemporary idea of justice, which underpins modern citizenship. Keechang Kim, one of the foremost experts on aliens in medieval law, makes this point with abundant clarity:

> For the Roman and mediaeval jurists, *ius personarum* was the very mechanism of unequal distribution of *libertas*. Their law (*ius*) was unequal, but it was grounded upon 'justice.' The point is that as long as justice is the basis of law, law cannot deliver liberty to all. Invariably, some will have it, some will not. Only when the law is truly grounded upon faith, can liberty be freely (*gratiis*) delivered to everybody in the name of law. Of course, 'everybody' here means an exclusive category within the bond of faith: that is, everybody within the mystic body.[23]

The mystic body politic is proclaimed as united by common faith and allegiance: once this becomes axiomatic, an alien not belonging to it is entirely out of the picture. The emergence of an individual with a personal rather than group-assigned identity and a life plan opens the door to the idea of citizenship as we know it today, and also enables a departure from the original tribalism of *ius sanguinis*. Modern citizenship is thus related to Pauline soteriology more directly than one would first presume. In approaching the promise of equality as necessarily bounded by the scope of the proclaimed holders of the status in a world where different citizenships are so dramatically unequal, it is essential to not accept any egalitarian claims of citizenship at face value. Although ideologically opposed to the antiquated idea of justice based on the presumption of inequality, inequality is *exactly* what contemporary citizenship embraces in practice. Every Ghanaian, Uzbek, or Ecuadorian—unlike the holders of the elite citizenships—would sense it with his skin. There is thus a huge gap between the reigning egalitarian ideology of citizenship and the contrarian boosting of global inequality that citizenship furthers in practice.

Contemporary citizenships have mostly been following *ius soli* in the Americas, Australia, and New Zealand and mostly *ius sanguinis* elsewhere, including in Europe. Again, this is a very rough generalization. A child of American parents born in Bahrain will acquire U.S. citizenship and a child of settled foreign residents of the UK will become British. Exceptions are crucially important. These concern, for instance, the number of generations through which the transfer of citizenship abroad is possible. While only allowed for two generations for the Danes, it is de facto unlimited for the Jewish Israelis.[24] Intergenerational transfer can move through the mother, the father, both parents, and other ancestors, including those born in territories that no longer form a part of the state granting nationality, such as Hungary prior to the Treaty of Trianon, for instance.[25]

An extremely complicated web of entirely arbitrary but constantly rationalized rules spans the whole world. The most authoritative database of these rules—EUDO Citizenship at the European University Institute in Florence—currently includes thirty different modes of citizenship acquisition,[26] no doubt conflating many distinct types, such as investment and donation citizenships, for instance, as analyzed by Kristin Surak.[27] The variety is overwhelming.

If you still think you are a proud citizen of your one country, you might want to double-check, as you may discover you are a holder of other surprising statuses, as an unfortunate Australian senator, Nick Xenophon, did recently, when he found that he was a British Overseas Citizen—a citizenship so disadvantageous, it does not even entitle the owner to live in the country of citizenship, the UK. It is a citizenship nevertheless, which can affect one's rights and obligations. In the case of Senator Xenophon, it potentially voided his ability to remain a senator of Australia, as the southern continent is among the very few countries that discriminate against dual nationals, barring them from holding high political office and thus mandating the random exclusion of a large number of

Australians from passive political rights. While even the president of the Australian Senate has been affected by the decision of the High Court of Australia in 2017, which barred dual citizens from elected office,[28] Senator Xenophon's situation was particularly irrational, given that his second citizenship comes with no rights in the UK—he can neither reside nor work in the territory of the British Isles.[29] The status he holds is largely meaningless, the Australian Court ruled,[30] allowing the gentleman to stay in the Australian Senate, but in obvious contradiction with the whole questionable idea behind the Australian norm the court was called to apply: once political rights in Australia are damaged by a citizenship issued, unavoidably, under foreign law, should it be up to Australia to decide how "real" and "meaningful" this citizenship is, as long as a foreign power designates it as such? Following *Re Xenophon* we know that one of the British citizenships is not good enough to harm an Australian's rights. What about, say, a Lybian citizenship? Or an Iraqi one? These are definitely "real," which does not make them more usable by any Australian senator than the British Overseas citizenship. At least the British Overseas citizenship status could be disposed of, should the Australian court be friendlier to its content. The truly worst off in contemporary Australia are those who cannot renounce their other citizenships, because of how foreign rather than Australian law regulates this. This means that a large number of Australians are de facto barred from political life on entirely irrational grounds, following Greek, Iranian, and Argentinian law, among others. It is most ironic that the operation of the Australian democracy is subjected—thanks to Australia's own High Court—to foreign law, over which Australia has no control and which is given a most drastic effect with the High Court's blessing: to deprive Australians of the right to be elected and govern themselves as a nation. The only exception here is the unlikely possibility of continuing the *Re Xenophon* line of telling other nations that their own citizenship is not serious enough: a dubious starting premise for rebuilding the torn political inclusiveness in the Australian democracy.

Faced with the complex and often unpredictable web of rules enabled by the absolute sovereignty that states around the world enjoy in the matters of nationality, as confirmed by Article 1 of the Hague Convention on Certain Questions Relating to the Conflict of Nationality Laws (1930), checking what your citizenship acquisition rules are before the birth of your child is fundamentally important, as these rules are frequently counterintuitive, to say the least. Article 1 of the Hague Convention states that "it is for each State to determine under its own law who are its nationals," which, in a world of more than two hundred authorities issuing citizenship around the globe, roughly translates into "anything is possible." To take the example of the Netherlands: if a child is born in the

Netherlands to a Dutch father and a foreign mother when the couple is not married, although the Netherlands is an *ius sanguinis* country, the child until very recently would not be Dutch if the father has not brought an official declaration of fatherhood *before* the birth of the child. If a Colombian couple has a child abroad, the child cannot claim Colombian nationality until the moment the parents ask for it and will not acquire it if they do not.[31] A child born in American Samoa will not be a U.S. citizen, acquiring a U.S. "non-citizen national" status instead, although American Samoa is a territory fully under the sovereignty of the United States. This unique colonial status of subjugation currently is reserved by the United States exclusively for American Samoans.[32]

Plentiful legal collisions can arise even at the moment of the automatic assignment of citizenship by birth. The rules here are quite basic: international law would normally limit the statelessness of children under the 1961 Convention on the Reduction of Statelessness, thus requiring states to follow the *ius soli* rule in the case of all children who have not acquired any nationality at birth.[33] A stateless child born in Belarus is a Belarusian citizen.[34] Though this works beautifully on paper, the rule can at the same time be both ignored and overused to questionable ends. The Persian Gulf boasts of large multigenerational stateless populations, as the Gulf Cooperation Council states do not comply with the demands of the strong international consensus against statelessness. Instead of giving citizenship to the local stateless, the *Bidūn*,[35] the Gulf States buy for them the nationality of the Comoros—a destitute African island nation at the bottom of all the development indexes. This awful practice is rendered even more problematic, as Atossa Araxia Abrahamian has shown, by the fact that those who disagree with how the Gulf sheiks run their autocracies can then easily be deported "back home" to the Comoros, getting a chance to use their new passport (a document they have never before been entitled to, as stateless, in their lives).[36] However appalling, one is bound to recognize that the practice of granting any citizenship to a stateless person in such a context is also obviously empowering for those *Bidūn* who are not politically outspoken: it is better to have any passport and be able to travel than have none at all, prevented from leaving the UAE no matter what.

Rather than entirely defied, as in the UAE, the international consensus on statelessness can also be complied with at the level of pretense. The Latvian state distributed the status of "non-citizens of Latvia," as opposed to citizenship, among roughly a third of its population, mostly of Jewish, Russian, and Ukrainian ancestry, but with no citizenship, claiming, quite bizarrely that "non-citizenship" does not amount to statelessness.[37] Although the number of the holders of the "non-citizen" status has fallen to 11 percent of the country's fast-shrinking population over the last two decades, children are still born with this status in the Latvian Republic.[38] At the other end of the spectrum are the children of the citizens of countries—such as Colombia cited earlier—that do not grant *ius sanguinis* citizenship automatically to those born outside the territory. In practical terms, this effectively means that a child born to Colombian parents anywhere in the world where international law on avoiding statelessness is respected will acquire the nationality of the place of birth in all cases where the parents refrain from registering the child as a Colombian citizen at a local consulate of Colombia.[39] Such refusals to register a child, although arousing quite some controversy in Europe, are completely legal. Moreover, they are also most logical in many cases, if the child's best interest is considered.

Anyone who tells you that the allocation of citizenships worldwide is logical and clear would thus not be telling the truth. At the macro level such a claim equals seeking logic in the perpetuation of the rigid pre-modern caste structures. At the micro level such a claim is problematic too. Local birth is good for Uruguayans but irrelevant to Germans; a tenured professorship in a local university is irrelevant to Germans, but was a key to immediate citizenship in Austria until 2008; "being active in the diaspora" is irrelevant to Austrians, but can make you a Pole; having a Lebanese mother is irrelevant to the Lebanese, but a Jewish mother, even without an Israeli citizenship, can make you an Israeli. The rules are truly diverse and the examples of this diversity are countless: what is taken for granted as best practice in one country can seem almost outrageous in another. All in all, however, it is crucial to realize that there cannot be a "worse" or a "better" method of assignment to a caste. It is the repugnant assumptions underlying the very rationale of a caste system that are intolerable.

But even the sheer diversity of regulation creates challenges. Not knowing the rules can result in surprises with deep implications for the life of the child and depends on the combination of the nationality rules in a child's country of birth and the countries of citizenship of the parents. A Moscow-born child of a Dane who himself was born to a naturalized father and lived outside of Denmark and a Jordanian mother could actually be Russian, unable to reside with the parents in Denmark without a residence permit or even enter the country without a visa. Jordan does not allow for *ius sanguinis* transfer of citizenship via the mother and Danish law—just as the law of several other Nordic countries is very restrictive on *ius sanguinis* citizenship transfers abroad.[40] Consequently, the child, born stateless in this case, will receive Russian citizenship by birth, even though Russia does not in general recognize *ius soli*. Similar cases are more common than one would expect, illustrating the randomness of citizenship assignment. In addition to producing surprises, they also cause the cumulation of nationalities. A child of a naturalized German friend of mine, a professor of Transylvanian-Jewish background and his British girlfriend with an Irish grandfather, born in New Haven, Connecticut, is of course American, British, German, Hungarian, Irish, Israeli, and Romanian. The number of such people is growing, also outside the Yale campus, contextualizing the meaning and significance of citizenship as a concept. Most crucially, however, the person is always claimed without any consent. An attempt to disagree, to defy authority claiming your allegiance can result, depending on the circumstances, in a court martial, a prison sentence, or internment in an insane asylum.[41] Formal renunciation can be very costly and difficult and will often be impossible.

As we have seen, 98 percent of the world's population never undergo a change in status that was initially assigned to them. However, although the most popular, assignment at birth is not the only way to acquire citizenship. The remaining 2 percent are worth looking at. Those acquiring citizenship after the initial assignment has occurred usually do it via one of the many forms of naturalization. Truly exceptional in the times of Georg Friedrich Händel, naturalization is now commonplace: only a handful of exceptional countries would make it de facto impossible, such as the Federated States of Micronesia or Israel. The rules of naturalization are no simpler or more intuitive than those for the acquisition of citizenship status by birth. Some are extremely complex: a special Act of Parliament is still required in Iceland to naturalize anyone. The same procedure as applied to Händel in eighteenth-century England was thus applied to the great piano virtuoso Vladimir Ashkenazy in the twentieth. Some naturalization rules were infinitely easier in the past. The German states of the Holy Roman Empire, in one example, used "presumed naturalization," as Andreas Fahrmeir reported. Residence in a new German state implied, for any foreign German, the acquisition of a new citizenship once the entry fees had been paid and a certain residence period lapsed.[42] Totalitarian regimes of the twentieth century would equally use assumed naturalization very broadly: those individuals unable to prove the possession of a foreign citizenship with valid documents were considered Soviet citizens in the Soviet Union amid Stalin's purges of the 1930s, as Eric Lohr documented.[43] A rudimentary variant—even if a much more benevolent one—of assumed naturalization is still found in some contemporary federations: in the United States a citizen of Connecticut who moves to Manhattan becomes a New Yorker.[44] The only difference is that it is now for free, while becoming a citizen of a prestigious and prosperous German state was very expensive indeed.

Naturalizations thus come in a remarkable variety of forms. The most common variant involves residence in the country for a certain period of time and passing a language and culture test as well as swearing an oath of allegiance to the country or the local real or imaginary ruler:

Elisabeth II, the Queen of New Zealand; the people of San Marino; or "Almighty God" himself,[45] if need be. Rules vary remarkably and are riddled with exceptions throughout. Officially, it takes five years to naturalize in Antigua and Barbuda, ten years in Italy, and seven years in Spain. In practice, however, Antiguan and Barbudan citizenship is bought overnight; Italy allows naturalization after two years of marriage to an Italian (changed from six months in the beginning of this century); and any citizen of a former colonial possession of Spain—from the Philippines to Argentina, but with the exception of the never formally decolonized Western Sahara—only requires two years of residence, while physical presence is not actually checked. The same goes for language: while Hungary seemingly requires it, speaking or understanding Hungarian is not indispensable in practice. Denmark, however, requires a near-native level, ensuring that two thirds of the applicants for naturalization, having spent many years in the country, fail all the same,[46] thus remaining both in *and* excluded, continuing their lives as before in broken Danish, English, and Mandarin and proving, yet again, the absurdity of the requirement they suffered from. Therefore it is not surprising that official exceptions become the rule in numerous cases. For example, as many people naturalize in Italy by residence as they do by marriage, and the percentage of naturalized Spaniards who do not come from the former Spanish colonies is tiny.[47]

The picture is further complicated by the fact that for residence to count for naturalization, it is not always simply legal residence, but a special settled or permanent residence that is required. The distinction is not in how you reside and what you do, but only and solely on the type of legal status you hold. As such, in the United States one needs a green card to naturalize, in the UK an indefinite leave to remain, and so on. The majority of foreigners reside in the country many years on non-immigrant visas before acquiring a green card, which means that the stated period to naturalization is much longer in practice, unless you win in the green card lottery organized by the U.S. government.[48] Interestingly, in the majority of cases legal residence does not translate into physical presence: doing business, studying, and sometimes continuously living abroad for a while would not affect it—legal residence is necessarily a legal fiction akin to citizenship; it is not necessarily an issue of fact. Rather, it is evolving into a right. Once legal residence is granted, it is up to the holder of this status to use her right to spend time in that jurisdiction. While many states have established minimal physical presence requirements, these often are not checked at all. Frequently, however, neither physical presence nor legal residence is required to acquire citizenship. This can apply, for instance, to those individuals who can trace their parentage to a citizen a number of generations back—the exact rules varying, again, by country. Such a semi-mythical ancestor, who died before your father (or your great-grandfather) was born, can ensure you are exempt from residency or any other requirement. Italy, in one example, created more than a million additional Italians in Latin America shortly after the change of the relevant law in 1992.[49] Israel is even more serious about ancestral bonds of course: *Aliyah* not only implies the entitlement of all the "Jews" to "return," but also exempts them from taxation for their worldwide income for ten years, making this option an attractive one indeed.[50]

Not only dead ancestors count, however. Family ties are another facilitator of naturalizations. A once-famous Soviet proverb summed it up quite well: "a Jewish wife is not a woman, but a means of transportation" given that only Jews and their spouses could leave the USSR, an otherwise sealed cage for its own people.[51] Spouses with the right documents can make your life much easier: naturalization residence times for family members are usually shorter, the fees lower, and other requirements laxer, as we have seen with Italy, for instance. Many countries, including the Netherlands and France, do not require family members to reside in the country at all, as long as they are officially registered as living for a certain period under the same roof as their citizen spouse, anywhere in the world. Needless to say, no one from the French embassy will show up at the door of your Jamaican family home before the day of your naturalization.

A separate subcategory of citizenship acquisition rules are those based on a collective sense of guilt for past crimes. Most of these rules are quite controversial. Spain and Portugal are the leaders of the pack here, "restoring" citizenship to the descendants of the Jews expelled from the Iberian peninsula by the *Reyes Católicos* in 1492, when Jews were made illegal following the "liberation" from Muslim rule. As Hans Ulrich Jessurun d'Oliveira has demonstrated, this means in practice that virtually anyone who can trace origins to those expelled is entitled to *both* Spanish and Portuguese citizenship.[52] No one is restoring anything to the expelled Muslims, ironically, or to the descendants of the Jews who converted to Christianity under duress. Such selective memory is the rule, rather than the exception:[53] Latvians who escaped the country's various occupations could get their citizenship back, while a large portion of the country's resident population became stateless upon independence, with their children still being born, in direct defiance of international law, bearing the status of "non-citizens of Latvia," as we have already seen.

Selective memory, perceived cultural affinity, and proclaimed identities go hand in hand as indispensable elements of state building: "*l'oublie et l'erreur historique*" as Ernest Renan memorably put it.[54] Many countries grant citizenship for "service to the diaspora"—such as Poland—or conversion to a particular set of beliefs, as

Israel does with Judaism[55] and the Stalinist Soviet Union did with communism. The latter rule helped, obliquely but truly, to unite Europe: the champion of the European idea, the French *directeur du plan*-to-be Monsieur Jean Monnet, desperate to wed his already married lover, brought her in 1934 to the Stalinist Soviet Union to get her to swear she was a communist and a believer in world revolution, the key conditions—besides useful connections in the government—for becoming a Soviet citizen at the time. Silvia, having become a Soviet citizen, then divorced her Italian husband—Monnet's former colleague, a subordinate in fact—and married the future father of Europe under Soviet law, which was much friendlier to women at a time when many Western European countries still refused to recognize the concept of divorce at all. The newlyweds left the USSR immediately after the ceremony.[56] Silvia, an Italian by birth, would later also become a French and U.S. citizen, as the family switched countries participating in shaping world affairs at the time.

Among the most curious cases of citizenship conferral is the symbolic elevation of the dead to the status, like the relatively recent granting of U.S. citizenship to "Mr. Lafayette"—Marquis de La Fayette that is[57]—or the proclamation that some Syrians who drowned in the Mediterranean were in fact Italians, to offer politicians an attractive photo opportunity with coffins covered by a flag, which the drowned would probably not have recognized.

Underlining the absurdity of such acts is the fact that the friends and family members of the drowned could not attend the ceremony, locked as they were behind bars at a detention center for illegal migrants.[58]

Christian Joppke, an intellectual leader in the sociology of citizenship, characterized the recent evolution of the rules informing the status of citizenship around the world as developing along the contrasting vectors of de-ethnicization and re-ethnicization. The first refers to the increasing proliferation and relatively easy naturalization rules, thus opening up "container societies." Increasingly many people can now become citizens by law of the states of their choosing. The second refers to the increased possibilities for citizens to retain the status connection to the state of origin of one's sometimes-remote ancestors, thus acquiring a full status of belonging in a society where one has never been, the language of which one does not speak, and the news of which one does not follow. These seemingly contradictory lines of development are fully in accord with the more general trend worldwide of making citizenship status less restrictive and more accessible, de facto and de jure, to previously excluded individuals and groups. Citizenship is thus becoming less totalitarian: a development that exposes a deep contradiction that goes to the essence of this abstract, hitherto always absolutely involuntary status. By becoming somewhat less totalitarian, citizenship, of course, is losing its relevance.

Change, Renunciation, and Cumulation

The status of citizenship traditionally has been absolute and irrevocable. Once acquired at birth, it sticks for life. In a world of inalienable allegiance, every naturalization abroad was akin to an attack on national sovereignty and public order. In such a world both a change in nationality and the cumulation of nationalities was viewed as undesirable and was made extremely difficult: the totalitarianism of citizenship was at its peak. This inflexible approach was built on an absolute denial of human agency, and eventually led to rising international tensions. Settler nations—in particular the United States—were overwhelmingly interested in the revision of the prevailing practice, dressing it, quite predictably, in the language of freedom and choice. The "old world" did not pay much attention, however: early nineteenth century saw the UK navy routinely collect all non-U.S.-born sailors aboard American merchant ships at sea, refusing to acknowledge any naturalization papers and punishing them for failing to honor their obligations under their perpetual and inalienable allegiance to the British king.[59] The tensions were only resolved with the 1870 Treaty between the two countries,[60] officially acknowledging the right to change allegiance. Concluding such agreements, the first of which entered into force in 1868, has been one of the core priorities of U.S. foreign policy, as Herzog has shown,[61] even though some states, like the Russian Empire, refused to go along with the U.S. approach and consistently ignored the U.S. citizenship of its (former) own subjects.[62]

The acknowledgment of the freedom to change citizenship came without a right to cumulate, however—a restriction that still remains in a fast shrinking number of jurisdictions, such as Japan, Kazakstan, and Slovakia. George Bancroft—the U.S. official behind the citizenship treaties with European nations—pointed to the prohibition of polygamy and applied—bizarrely from a contemporary perspective—the same reasoning to the cumulation of nationalities. He famously argued that states should "as soon tolerate a man with two wives as a man with two countries; as soon bear with polygamy as that state of double allegiance which common sense so repudiates that it has not even coined a word to express it."[63] Such empty moralizing was bound to go and the world has, expectedly, moved in the direction of the late Sir James Goldsmith's wise comment that "who marries a lover creates a vacancy." Changing citizenship—just like holding one—has graduated into a right, albeit as unenforceable as these frequently are, under international law, which proclaims very much while resting on the benevolence of other legal systems to attain compliance. Thus the UN's Universal Declaration of Human Rights not only mentions a right to nationality in Article 15, but also states that "no one shall be arbitrarily deprived of his nationality nor denied the right to change his nationality." The right "to change" implies of course a right to seek naturalization and, equally important, a right to renounce the previously held nationality, should this be desired or required.[64]

In practice, even though the majority of states would now at least allow a person to leave to seek naturalization elsewhere, several countries—none among the most highly developed—still refuse to permit renunciations.[65] The drama of this is well known, even beyond Obama-inspired Trump travel bans, which initially would have excluded from visa-free travel to the United States all those, inter alia, who hold the citizenships of "rogue states," including Yemen, Syria, and Iran, no matter which other countries could also vouch for the persons in question.[66] Most problematic, such bans ignored the actively held citizenships shaping a person's day-to-day life, in favor of a dormant "terror" status acquired through a grandfather born in a country that the unwelcome foreigner has never visited, but the citizenship of which can never be renounced. Deprived of any logic and incapable of improving security, such populist measures parading as "anti-immigration," in practice merely poison lives, stigmatizing law-abiding people for no reason, as is often the case in citizenship and immigration regulation.

A dormant citizenship of a foreign land you did not know you had could have more dire repercussions than making a Luxembourgian with Iranian roots queue for a U.S. visa that would otherwise not be required, or ejecting a

British Overseas Citizen from a senatorial race in Australia. The current practice in international law dictates that a person in one of the states of her nationality should be treated merely as a national of that state; other citizenships evaporate in the eyes of the law. This allows Iran and other similarly eager countries to harass people who have never relied on these ancestral nationalities and only acquired them because they could not be renounced. The same applies to those who moved on with their lives from their country of birth. So when Dr. Serkan Golge, an American NASA scientist of Turkish descent, was taken hostage by the Erdoğan government in 2016 following the failed coup attempt in the country, U.S. consular officials were not even allowed to see him: his U.S. citizenship had thus de facto evaporated in a Turkish prison when it was needed most.[67] This practice is fiercely contested by the United States, Canada, EU nations, and many others, but still affects a large number of people in a desperate situation.[68] It would thus still appear that even citizenships one does not use can become sources of liability, and not being able to renounce them obviously is capable of producing negative effects for several generations. In essence, this is just one of the emanations of the myth of the equal dignity of all citizenships, which, when implemented, does nothing but rupture lives.

Just as not being able to renounce a citizenship can objectively run counter to the interests of the citizen, being forced to renounce—another way of depriving the citizen of the right to decide—can often be as bad, if not worse. This is because, as we will discuss in chapter 3, the status of citizenship is connected to a bundle of rights, including— most important of all—the right to enter and remain in the country as long as you want and to work there. Giving up these rights in the context of acquiring a new nationality limits one's horizon of opportunities while serving no productive purpose, unless you come from a country that does not prize the rule of law, such as Turkey, which will happily take you hostage. This is particularly harmful when the renunciation requirement is applied to those who hold two or more citizenships from the moment of birth. The states of nationality would then offer a person the opportunity to choose "the right side of the self" and to get rid of rights enjoyed in other states: the pointlessness and violence of this approach to reinstating the myth of national uniqueness, practiced by a handful of markedly nationalistic countries, is obvious. Many Japanese reaching maturity are told every year that they are no longer worthy of equality and rights in the country, should they opt to keep their German, U.S., or Korean citizenships. Any allusion to "choice" offered to these Japanese kids is of course hypocritical and misplaced, akin to offering the "choice" to unlearn a mother tongue or relinquish important rights without getting anything in return.

There are at least two key arguments against such renunciation requirements that go beyond a straightforward virtue of respecting the individual choice of the person in question, which should be the starting point, instead of stripping her of rights for no compelling reason.

Peter Spiro, the key authority on multiple nationalities in the world today, and famously an American, German, and at least potentially an Israeli (with a disclaimer of "not being sure"), adopted a convincing human rights-inspired approach to multiple nationality cumulation: no country's citizenship law should endeavor to curtail the rights of citizens elsewhere.[69] The good news is that this is the global trend today. Over the last thirty years, most countries in the world have come to tolerate the cumulation of numerous nationalities—some historically, like the UK, some since the 1960s, like the United States, some only since the end of the twentieth century, like Mexico and Italy. Denmark, which amended its law in 2016, is among the latest additions to the growing list. Requiring anyone to renounce foreign nationalities is a limitation of the extra-jurisdictional rights of that person, sometimes cutting to the heart of his or her self-identification; most importantly, it solves nothing whatsoever in our global world: a cruel jest to no end. The international consensus that used to oppose the toleration of multiple nationalities has thus reversed, as important research by Vink, de Groot, and Luk shows (figure 3). Nationality cumulation is a human right, Spiro argues.

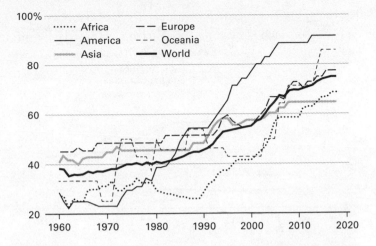

Figure 3 Dual nationality toleration around the world
Source: M. P. Vink, G.-R. de Groot, and N. C. Luk, "MACIMIDE Global
Expatriate Dual Citizenship Dataset" (Harvard, 2015), https://doi:10.7910/
DVN/TTMZ08.

The other and probably most powerful argument
against intolerance of the cumulation of nationalities has
been offered by the U.S. Supreme Court in *Afroyim v. Rusk*.
In the words of Mr. Justice Black, writing for the Court,
"In our country the people are sovereign and the Government
cannot sever its relationship to the people by taking
away their citizenship."[70] Countless countries around the
world have followed the "sovereign citizen" and the human
rights arguments, either explicitly or implicitly. The
automatic loss of citizenship upon naturalization abroad

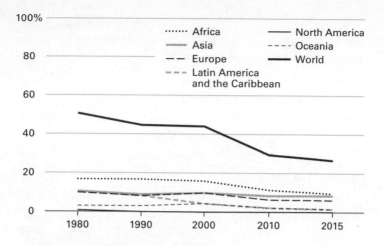

Figure 4 Global evolution of the laws on the automatic loss of nationality upon naturalization abroad
Source: M. P. Vink, G.-R. de Groot, and N. C. Luk, "MACIMIDE Global Expatriate Dual Citizenship Dataset" (Harvard, 2015), https://doi:10.7910/DVN/TTMZ08.

has particularly dramatically diminished around the world in recent decades, as figure 4 demonstrates. The age of citizenship's uniqueness is over.[71]

Sexism and the Subjugation of Women

The main source of the cumulation of citizenships is not naturalization abroad, but the birth of children to mixed-nationality couples, something that could not result in the cumulation of nationalities at all until recently, leaving the children of mixed couples mononational. We come to yet another of what were the core functions of citizenship until the very end of the twentieth century: citizenship status had traditionally been an effective legal-political device for the systemic subjugation of women. We will see this in the chapters that follow at the level of rights: women only got the right to vote at the federal level in Switzerland in 1971.[72] They are subjected to systemic discrimination in Saudi Arabia and a handful of other totalitarian regimes. The same applies at the level of duties: women are still often denied the authority to make decisions even about their own bodies, thus denied dignity in the name of procreating for the nation—the core duty of any woman in the classical understanding of citizenship. Before moving to rights and duties, however, which will be discussed in chapters 3 and 4, the masculine bias of citizenship needs to be clarified at the level of operation of the status of citizenship already.

Until well into the twentieth century, only men enjoyed a citizenship status that they could pass to their children. Moreover, only men enjoyed citizenship independently of their marital status. The very first exceptions to these harshly exclusionary rules only appear around the end of World War I. The standard approach in citizenship law and policy around the world was that women, while able to bear a child, were never able to produce a new citizen. Given that citizenship is an abstract status, in the eyes of the law it was insufficient for a woman holding the status to give birth to a human being and thereby endow the newborn with citizenship. Moreover, once marrying a foreigner, a woman would lose her original citizenship and follow her husband's.[73] It is difficult for us, at this point—even with a handful of countries still sticking to this indefensible approach—fully to fully appreciate the overwhelming extent of humiliation that citizenship has caused throughout its entire history until the latter half of the twentieth century. All the world round, citizenship has traditionally been (and tends to remain so in many places) de facto a status for *men only*. The subjugation of women is thus an essential part of the citizenship story, which must be taken fully into account when citizenship is analyzed. In fact, this is one of the most consistent features throughout the story of citizenship. All the core presumptions of citizenship have changed since the days of Aristotle—equal human worth, individualism, and rights all have no parallels in ancient Greece—only the idea that a woman is not really a citizen has remained. It took brave souls and enormous sacrifices to reverse this vital aspect of citizenship.

Paula Marckx, a journalist in Antwerp and a qualified pilot for a cargo airline specializing in the transport of diamonds, decided to raise a child alone, without a husband or partner.[74] When the time came to register the newborn, the Belgian clerk at the local communal office asked the

Citizenship has traditionally been (and tends to remain so in many places) de facto a status for *men only*.

mother to sign a judicial declaration—"a pure formality" for the proper adoption of the child by the Belgian state. Without it, Marckx was told, the child would not be recognized as Belgian, since the father was unknown and the mother, under a Belgian law that reflected the European consensus at the time, could not pass on her citizenship to her offspring. Marckx refused, finding this practice humiliating, and lost her case in *all* the Belgian courts, only to have her rights upheld by the European Court of Human Rights in Strasbourg—the highest all-European jurisdiction in the area of human rights, which found in 1979 that the practice was discriminatory.[75]

Belgium was not among the last to change the law, as many states around the world still prohibit women from passing on nationality—Lebanon, Jordan, Somalia, and Swaziland, for example. The most notable break with this traditional element of citizenship came from Soviet Russia, which did in 1917—right after the revolution—what Belgium was pushed to do by the highest court in Europe when it amended its law in 1988, to grant full citizenship to women, including the right to pass it on. Once a woman emerges as a more or less equal citizen (on paper at least) in terms of legal status, practical consequences, including improved access to formerly "male" professions and education follow: the promise of equality does its job. In 1924, the first woman ambassador was officially appointed: Soviet Russia's Madame Kollontai introduced herself to the

King of Norway, causing a stir. The press branded her a "Valkyrie of the revolution" and even an "anti-Christ," also ascribing her "horrid views in relation to marriage and love," as she remembers in her *Autobiography of a Sexually Emancipated Communist Woman*,[76] instead of focusing on her competence and achievements.

Not being able to pass citizenship on to their children has traditionally been one of two key ways of denying women access to the full status of citizenship worldwide. The second, probably even more dramatic, is denying a woman the ability to remain a citizen following marriage to a foreigner. Crucially, this incapacity of women to remain themselves in the eyes of the law has, just like denying women the right to pass citizenship on to their offspring, continued well into the last century all around the world, and is still present in some societies. Turkmen law today, instead of making foreigners out of Turkmen women deemed unfaithful to the nation, makes foreign husbands pay a bridal tax to the treasury of Turkmenistan, now set at USD 50,000—around fifteen times the average annual income in the country.[77] Marriage becomes impossible before the tax is paid, unless the lady corrects her wayward-ness and chooses a Turkmen man: marrying those guys is free.[78] Women thus emerge as effectively the property of the state and are viewed in the gas-rich dictatorship as an economic asset, while their faithfulness to the Turkmen nation is at the same time ensured: who would have USD

50,000 to spare? However outrageous, this approach is in essence no different from that of Belgium or the Netherlands of a generation ago, in that it steeply disqualifies women from the rights enjoyed by male citizens. One positive thing to note about the Turkmen lawmakers is that their approach is of course better and obviously more just than an outright ban on marrying any foreigners, which many countries have enforced throughout history.[79]

The progressive reform of the approaches to women citizens that make Turkmenistan exceptional began in the United States, where the law was changed in 1922 following a high-profile case of denaturalization of a famous communist activist, Emma Goldman, "the High Priestess of Anarchism,"[80] who lost her citizenship after the naturalization of her husband was annulled. His retroactive denaturalization was used as a pretext to kick Emma out of the country as punishment for political speech: a great way around the First Amendment for the U.S. authorities. This saga, brilliantly retold by Patrick Weil, so obviously political and so dramatically unjust, swayed public opinion in the United States and as of 1922 gave American women a chance to remain precisely that: American women, even after marrying a foreigner, or for those naturalized, after the naturalization of their husband had been retroactively annulled. Women have remained citizens after marrying a foreigner in the UK since 1948, in Germany since 1953, and in the Netherlands since 1985.

The most dramatic stories of women who lost their citizenship through marriage came from the racist countries with extensive colonial possessions. "Colonials" usually were never citizens in the strict sense of the word, as they were given a different status in the law of the empires, steeply inferior to the status held by the citizens of the *metropole*. This practice still survives in the United States. As we have already seen, in American Samoa the United States distributes a U.S. nationality without citizenship, depriving Americans of political rights based on race, whatever the official justification.[81] The United States is among the last Western democracies doing this.

Looking at another empire, Christiaans and Schrover documented the very common instances of women who considered themselves Dutch, only to discover that they were actually either colonial "inlanders" or stateless when they applied for Dutch passports to leave Indonesia, unwilling to stay in the former colony and fleeing the turmoil of the newly independent country along with 400,000 others.[82] It is heartbreaking to see what happened to women who crossed the legally mandated racial line and fell in love with those who were, although subjects of the same sovereign, subjugated as racially inferior by law. Having chosen a life with the holders of an inferior status, Dutch women lost their white privilege and were no longer treated as belonging to the mother-nation, notwithstanding the fact that, obviously, both the citizenship of the Netherlands and the colonial status of inlanders had been created by *the same state*. In this case, marrying a foreigner was in fact marrying an inlander, a legally inferior national, crossing the race divide, which was policed by the Dutch authorities very strictly.

The irony of this policing, of course, is that in contrast, all colonial women had to be available to white Dutch males holding full citizenship status.[83] Moreover, colonial women would become fully Dutch citizens upon marrying a Dutchman, losing their colonial status. The French state, while denying women full personhood in law in the same way at the time, was more "equitable" regarding their offspring—and thus potentially even more racist. A child born of a colonial *sujet* family to a French woman would be presented to a judge, who would then decide based on cultural factors and baptismal records—read the color of the skin of the child—whether to make an exception and allow the child to become French. This is just one example from Emmanuelle Saada's groundbreaking research on the pillars of sexism and racism on which the republican citizenship tradition in France was founded.[84]

Racism and Imperialism

Citizenship has always been racist in essence.[85] This essential characteristic has admittedly been fading lately at the state level, but at the same time has been reinforced dramatically in interstate relations. The holders of the former colonial citizenship statuses are now confined to foreign states, often but not necessarily completely subjugated economically by former colonizers. Such states provide the former colonials with citizenships that are a liability, rather than true bundles of rights—remember the Pakistani we started with. All the data on HDI, freedom of travel, and the development of the democratic institutions aside, it takes strolling through a Western airport with a Comorran passport in hand to see that, more frequently than not, a former colonial's status means that person is an outcast. A Comorran in the CDG or LAX is not your "Englishman in New York." Decolonization and its aftermath have in fact upgraded the racial divide in the area of citizenship by confining the majority of the former colonial inferiors to "their own states," which are behind impenetrable visa walls, while citizenship of the former colonial masters offers an image of a world that is absolutely open: a Frenchman can travel to 173 countries, no questions asked, while an Algerian—a resident before the separation in 1962 of a fully incorporated part of France and an important producer of premium French wine—may travel to forty-eight mostly underdeveloped and dangerous territories.

Former colonials are not really welcome: the law of the former empires proves this basic point overwhelmingly.

The majority of the former colonies are behind steep visa walls and virtually no former colonials enjoy unconditional rights to settle in the former metropole.[86] Even the countries that were infinitely more centralized than the classical empires of the nineteenth century have produced such divides. The debate about introducing visas for Central Asians continually rumbles on in Russia[87] and has been concluded to the detriment of the citizens of the former colonies in the UK, France, the United States, and Portugal (with the notable exception of Brazil, where the centers of power reversed).

Although never framed in this way in law, the boundary here is unquestionably the one corresponding to the pigmentation of the skin of those who are not welcome. Those who shared the second-rate status of the "natives"— either de jure or de facto—in the Empires controlling the world before decolonization, came to enjoy—not surprisingly—a second-rate citizenship compared with the status of the former colonizers. Any criticism of the status quo is foreclosed by the core biases of citizenship discussed at the beginning of this chapter, especially the mantra of the equal dignity of citizenship of all the most atrociously underperforming—at times genocidal—states combined with the fables of "freedom" and "self-determination." Thus on paper, the second-rate former colonial citizenships are proclaimed to be as dignifying as the statuses distributed by the most developed nations topping the

HDI rankings. The argument "but they are free at least" should be deployed with caution in this context: many of the countries in question are too far removed from any possible ideal of political liberation and citizen empowerment to take such glorious proclamations seriously.[88]

The situation in the area of economic development, which has direct bearing on citizenship in the context of the prominence of spatial inequalities in today's world, is worse still. Milanovic discusses the situation of some nations—using the Democratic Republic of Congo and Madagascar as examples—where the income levels have gone down even since the moment of decolonization, currently standing at the levels they had eighty or ninety years ago, meaning a century of development has been entirely lost.[89] That racist subjugation rather than liberation has been among the core functions of citizenship, however, is beyond any reasonable doubt.

We have seen that women were de facto deprived not only of a room, but also of a nationality of their own,[90] and with racism it seems to have been worse, since plenty of countries made *ius soli* conferral of nationality or naturalization, or both, directly dependent on the color of one's skin. This regime was most elaborate and strict in the United States, Canada, Australia, and South Africa, but many other nations followed. The United States would simply not allow anyone of Chinese, Indian, or Japanese ancestry to naturalize for a large part of the twentieth century. Scholars and judges spoke of "inferior races" and the law in force excluded these entirely, outright prohibiting those proclaimed to belong to such races from entering the territory.[91] Having a darker complexion was thus regarded to be deeply un-American, with no other factors considered. Yet, who is "white" and who is not was a deeply esoteric legalistic matter depending on the law of the jurisdiction concerned, as we have seen, changing radically as one traveled from one state to another. The law was only changed in 1943 for the Chinese and 1952 for the Japanese, adding a general nondiscrimination provision in 1965 as a follow-up of the human rights movement.[92] That said, all children born in the United States, due to the strict application of the *ius soli* rule, were still American citizens. This is what *apartheid* South Africans abhorred, creating from 1976, a number of "ancestral homelands" on paper for the "non-white" population and proclaiming these to be independent states, assigning the majority of the population of the country to the newly invented citizenships of such Bantustans.[93] The international community refused to recognize any of these lands, but the fact that such "states" were phony did not deter South Africa from treating their "citizenship" seriously internally.[94] All citizens of South Africa who were not of European ancestry thus became foreigners in their own country. This had been the situation in Australia, too: de facto the aboriginals only received citizenship following the 1967 referendum.[95]

Racism has traditionally been a general founding prerequisite of citizenship status, of course, rather than merely a settler-colonialist phenomenon, even though the settler-colonial context is where it became most pronounced and publicized. Some newly decolonized states in the latter half of the twentieth century learned the lessons of racism from their former oppressors very well. Europeans were no longer welcome; neither were former citizens of Indian descent and sometimes also black Africans from different clans and tribes. The stories of mass deportations and the devastation racism inflicted on the African continent are well known. South Africa installed visa walls for all its neighbors, and *gastarbeiters* there are often subjected to gruesome pogroms. Nigeria deported *all* foreign workers in 1983, claiming they were illegal.[96] Tanzania, Uganda, Zimbabwe, Mozambique, and other African nations provided abundant ugly examples of mass racist violence against "non-black" populations, using race as a justification for mass looting and murder during the brutal initial stages of postcolonial decline, with cannibal-dictators, phony emperors, and rulers for life— the world described so well in the travel writings of V. S. Naipaul. Still today, citizenship is de facto race-specific in China, numerous African Nations, and the Arab world, producing statelessness and alienation. The UAE citizenship law requires non-GCC (Gulf Cooperation Council) citizens to reside in the country for thirty years prior to naturalization, as opposed to GCC citizens' many-times-shorter term.[97] Contemporary citizenship law in Liberia and Sierra Leone is simpler still: you need to be of "Negro descent" to acquire citizenship from birth. Moreover, Article 27(b) of the constitution of Liberia "in order to preserve, foster, and maintain the positive Liberian culture, values, and character" makes it impossible for those who are not "Negroes" to hold the citizenship of that country.[98]

Racists claim that those belonging to the "race" they happen to ascribe themselves to are better than those belonging to other races. The unhelpfulness of such a worldview is exposed best when its adherents attack those belonging—in the racists' own understanding—to the same race, and would still humiliate and dehumanize such people on racist grounds. This is where citizenship has always come in handy. One of the most telling examples spanning a large part of the twentieth century is the treatment of British subjects from the Indian subcontinent in the United States, Australia, South Africa, and Canada. Lawmakers faced an important dilemma, as they were stuck between racist unrest on the one hand—especially in California, where the people made it clear that Indians were not welcome, just like the Chinese and the Japanese—and the "race theory" of the day on the other. As Justice Southerland stated in *Bhagat Singh Thind*, Indians, although they could scientifically belong to the "Caucasian race" just like white Americans, had to be treated as if they were not white based on the "common" understanding.[99] "White" and "black" emerged as legal terms of art having little to do with the skin color even before the fall of race "science."[100] To remain racist meant to defy the theory of race, which racists officially preached. This is exactly what Congress had done, adding to the race-based exclusion of the Chinese and the Japanese from settlement and citizenship by naturalization a new, "purely geographical" exclusion by birth place specifically designed for the Indians, who were "scientifically" "white," which Sherally Munshi has so thoroughly documented.[101] Interestingly, the British colonial masters of the Indians— holding the same citizenship of course, and traveling on identical Indian Empire documents—did not see this limitation applied to them by U.S. authorities.

In summary, racism was one of the core features of citizenship worldwide until well into the second half of the twentieth century. Although the trend has been reversed at a global scale—at least in law—especially throughout the countries with the highest levels of development, including all of the former colonial settler nations, many states around the world still connect the legal status of citizenship to race. A different trend is observable between states: the majority of the former colonial subjects hold the statuses of citizenship distributed by former colonies. The majority of these citizenships are substantially inferior to those of their former colonizers. Furthermore, global naturalization figures demonstrate that citizenship's turn away from racism observable in the laws of most nations probably has not actually found its way into practice: not many former colonial subjects actually naturalize in the global north, where citizenships are of the highest quality, compared with the migrants from the already relatively rich countries, such as Brazil, China, Israel, Mexico, and Russia, whose citizens would frequently pursue naturalization for the perceived prestige of a passport from one of the most developed nations, rather than in order actually to move to the United States, Canada, or European nations.[102]

Deprivation of Status

In addition to the rules on the acquisition of citizenship, it is equally important to look at the rules behind *deprivation* of citizenship in order to understand the essence of this status and the practicalities of its functioning. The story of deprivation is obviously connected in the most direct way to the grant of the status of citizenship itself. Sometimes the line between the two is very thin indeed: illegality is an outcome of state policy on citizenship resulting from deprivation of citizenship or sometimes a non-extension of citizenship de facto amounting to deprivation. Consider President Trump's rescission in September 2017 of the DACA (Deferred Action for Childhood Arrivals) immigration policy: at least eight hundred thousand young people who do not have any other home but the United States were made potentially illegal. Unless the president is overruled, they will have to relocate to countries alien to them, simply because the United States chose not to extend to them the status of citizenship in the first place, in defiance of the basic logic of preserving the objective home of hundreds of thousands of Americans, who are now arbitrarily being punished for no personal wrongdoing. The state's task is precisely to ensure that its population has appropriate documentation, since illegalities are created uniquely by state policy. Consider Italy: exclusion there is much more acute than in the United States, since children born in the country to foreign parents do not become Italians—there is no *ius soli* to help them. In effect, all the children born to foreign couples are potentially illegal and subject to deportation, unlike *all* children born in the United States. The United States thus possesses a more just system, objectively at least, judging by the numbers: the majority of children present in any country are born there, not brought there.

Citizenship deprivation is not always simply racist, as with the case of DACA young people, the majority of whom are not coming from Finland or Norway. In addition to providing a way to reinforce and perpetuate prejudice, deprivation is also deployed to instill fear and to police speech and opinions. Deprivation of citizenship to police speech and beliefs was very popular around the world throughout the twentieth century, and practiced beyond the United States, in countless other countries, from the Soviet Union to the Third Reich. For example, Emma Goldman, the "high priestess of anarchism" mentioned earlier, found herself in Eastern Europe without her U.S. citizenship despite a whole adult life lived in U.S. politics after being stripped of her American citizenship. The Soviet Union held the dubious laurels of the leading jurisdiction among those practicing political citizenship deprivation, having denaturalized pretty much all the Imperial period elites, at times sending away whole ocean steamers packed with newly stateless scientists, poets, and philosophers.[103] Indeed, the exodus from Russia was so large in scale that it led to the invention of the Nansen passport—the first document given to stateless refugees, and is behind the thinking that gave rise to the Geneva Convention currently in force.[104] The Soviet activism in unmaking the former Russian subjects gave the world numerous stateless notable personalities, from Chagall to Diaghilev, Kandinsky, Nabokov, Rachmaninoff, Sikorsky, Stravinsky, and countless others. The situation of the stateless was dramatically precarious (just as it remains now): when the main character in Nabokov's *Mary* leaves his papers in a tram, our heart is broken. We understand that love is not possible.

Many did very well, however—from winning Nobel Prizes, such as the stateless author Ivan Bunin, to helping establish a modern legal system in Turkey, such as former member of the Russian State Duma, Sadri Maksudi Arsal, the illustrious advisor to Atatürk and the author of the history of Turkish law. The exiled were omnipresent in Hollywood, literature, industry, and the arts, providing a vivid illustration of the problematic underlying rationale for belief in the indispensable dignity of citizenship.

Political nationality deprivation is not as bad, however, compared with the purely racist annulments of citizenship that minorities including the Roma and the Jews endured under the Third Reich. These abhorrent policies mirrored in their logic the racist non-extension of citizenship to the "inferior races" elsewhere in the world by the European empires and the United States, which supplied the essential element of the global order of the day even if this was not always spelled out in racist terms (as we have also seen with the Indians in Canada, South Africa, and the United States).[105] Similarly, the Empire of Japan used the pretext of the place of origin registration to humiliate Korean subjects,[106] while the Soviet Union relied on the notion of "enemy peoples" for internal mass deportations.[107] The Nuremberg Laws of September 15, 1935, divided the citizenry of the Third Reich into citizens and non-Aryans. The latter were only allowed the obligations of citizenship. The unjustifiable racist distinction between different categories of subjects, well known in the world of empires from France to the Netherlands and the UK and still enforced in the case of U.S. "non-citizen nationals" in American Samoa today, was thus implemented in the heart of Europe. Deprivation of citizenship was the first step toward dehumanization of the German Jews.

As with anywhere else in the world where racism has been deployed as an argument, the "scientific" definition of race employed in the context of annulling German citizenship could not withstand the most basic logical scrutiny. As Ingo Müller explained, a "Jew" under the law was someone who was one-quarter Jewish, the Jewishness of the grandparents determined through checking their religious observance, nothing else.[108] Just as with the British dominions and the U.S. lawyers working on the exclusion of Indians, the absurdity of the arguments used to discriminatory ends was clear in Germany too. Those who believed in science tried to interpret racist law in the context of the race research of the time, which led to curious encounters between racist hatred and quasi-scientific reason. Hans Ulrich Jessurun d'Oliveira cites a curious example concerning Dr. Hans Calmeyer, who saved thousands of Dutch Jews by reclassifying them using "scientific evidence" following the arguments of the preeminent Dutch race scholars of the day, based on craniometrics and other contemporary scientific methods. The conclusions were that the Sephardic Jews were not necessarily the "Jews" that German race theory had in mind.[109] Law, using science as a pretext for arbitrary discrimination, cannot be disproved by science, however: Calmeyer's approach was overturned and only 30,000 out of 140,000 Dutch Jews survived the occupation.[110]

The end of World War II did not end statelessness for reasons of ethnic persecution and political duress: the Beneš decrees stripped millions of the Czechoslovak Germans of citizenship and robbed them of their country,[111] causing 15,000–30,000 of them to lose their lives.[112] The Soviet Union continued to put intellectuals perceived as dangerous on one-way flights. Japan stripped of their status all the former citizens resident in this radically shrunken country who were proclaimed to be of "Korean origin." Given that "Korea"—which many of these people had never visited—amounted to a choice between two dictatorships at war with each other, many descendants of Japanese citizens residing in Japan are still stateless today as a result of this policy.[113]

Some great personalities were born stateless or remained stateless for a very long time. Thus, E. M. Cioran, the author of *The Trouble with Being Born*, lived in melancholy in Paris and refused to naturalize, just like Mr. Wenceslas de Lobkowicz, who rose to the rank of Director General in the European Commission, and was the only stateless person in the history of the European Union to hold such a key position until the Czech Republic returned his citizenship and family properties upon the fall of the Berlin Wall. Alexander Grothendieck, a revolutionary in pure mathematics and professor at *Institut des hautes études scientifiques*, inherited statelessness from his parents and cherished it on principle. The Soviet Union used to deprive of citizenship anyone who wished to move abroad permanently, annulling their passport at the border. For those who were allowed a temporary trip, however, "unauthorized non-return from abroad" was a criminal offense against the state punishable grotesquely by capital punishment and later, a long jail term.[114]

The exclusionary trend only intensified in the context of decolonization, when skin color or opinions led to the exile of hundreds of thousands.[115] States have traditionally been at liberty to deprive individuals and groups of citizenship for sexist, religious, political, and racist reasons. Indeed, ethnic and religious homogeneity has been one of the key elements of classical nation-building. Although the legality of such practices is now dubious, states eagerly use this liberty still, to which the examples of Latvian "Russian speakers," the Slovenian erased, the Bhutani Lhotsampas,[116] Myanmar's Rohingya,[117] Dominicans "of Haitian origin,"[118] Indian muslims in Assam,[119] and countless other groups can testify. According to UNHCR, there are still roughly ten million stateless people around the world today. This is a conservative estimate: the figure could be much higher.[120] That said, while this figure reflects the reality that at least this number of people have no official status of nationality ascribed to them by any state, the figure fails to capture the actual drastic differences between different citizenships in the world. Holding some of these, although nominally permitting you to tick the citizenship box on paper, in practice amounts to de facto statelessness, since the status can be so poor in quality in terms of the rights and protections it grants, that it is no better—indeed, possibly worse—than statelessness. Consider being Syrian, Papuan, or Central African today.

Splitting states causes particular challenges, creating a conflict between purely legal realities—the newly created citizenships—and the actual lived experience of rights, duties, and expected identities. The splitting up of Yugoslavia produced seven different citizenships, as Igor Štiks reports, many of them mutually intolerant and installing lines of exclusion cutting through established communities and families.[121]

While the 1961 Convention on the Reduction of Statelessness and other international law prohibit "arbitrary deprivation of nationality," there are numerous exceptions to this rule, related mostly to the acquisition of the status by deception—via concealing the true identity, a marriage of convenience, or buying it with dirty funds. The most widely justified example of citizenship deprivation in the contemporary world, however, is the annulment of the citizenship of suspected terrorists. Here, the countries of the world are divided. At one end of the spectrum is the UK, where citizenship is annulled if the "Secretary of State is satisfied that the person has done anything seriously prejudicial to the vital interests [of the UK]"[122]—probably the weakest test today.[123] No US-inspired sovereign citizenship is in sight in Brexit-Britain: citizenship of the UK can be lost at any moment. At the other end of the spectrum is the United States, where citizenship deprivation is out of question. It is important, however, that unlike their British counterparts, the U.S. authorities are authorized by the rules of engagement currently in force to *kill* Americans abroad suspected of terrorist activity.[124]

Links with the Issuing State

The rules on citizenship change constantly around the world: the UK law on nationality has been changed a number of times over the last hundred years; the Dutch, French, and Italian laws have as well, to give just a handful of examples. States around the world simply decide based on the dominant prejudices of the time or based on what appears to be in their interests in terms of financial or other gains from the body of citizens combined with the reinforcement of the key prejudices in society. *Ius soli* is introduced when a state is interested in tapping into the potential of the native-born resident foreign population to reinforce a conscript army. *Ius sanguinis* is introduced when empowering the descendants of emigrants to vote is seen as potentially beneficial to the party in power—as happened recently with Italy, Hungary, and many other places and will be discussed in chapter 5. Dual nationality is prohibited when the state reacts, unreasonably, to a neighboring state extending nationality to its resident ethnic minorities, as was the case with Slovakia in 2010,[125] or tries to limit naturalizations, which is the case with Germany and its "Turks" many of whom have never been to Turkey.[126]

The effects of these changes, while absolute in the internal sphere of law of each state, can sometimes be limited internationally. The citizens of Kosovo, while possessing a status that is fine under Kosovo law, would not be Kosovars in Serbia, Spain, the Russian Federation, or any other state not recognizing the country.[127] Conversely, international practice also teaches us that the disappearance of a country as a result of illegal annexation does not unmake a citizen residing abroad: Austrians living in the United States at the time of the Anschluss could still naturalize as Austrians. Moreover, they were exempt from immigration regulations.[128] The Czechoslovak citizenship of Count Richard von Coudenhove-Kalergi—a famous Austrian-Japanese promoter of the unification of Europe and a real-life inspiration behind Victor László in Casablanca[129]—was recognized throughout World War

II by the Allied Powers.[130] It is an established principle of international law that the distribution of the occupier's citizenship among the population of the occupied territory does not produce legal effects internationally.[131] Unfortunately, contemporary examples of this seemingly archaic rule are at hand: the newly created "Russians" on the Crimean peninsula cannot rely on their citizenship abroad in the EU, in one example. Any Russian passport issued in the occupied territory should be considered invalid and no visas can be affixed to it.[132]

Some cases, however, are less straightforward—and here is where international law becomes unhelpful. In the 1955 case of *Nottebohm* the International Court of Justice (ICJ) in The Hague ruled that Friedrich Nottebohm, who lost all his numerous possessions in Guatemala as a result of being mistakenly taken for a German by the Guatemalan authorities and thus categorized as an "enemy alien" and illegally imprisoned by the U.S. military after Guatemala entered World War II on the U.S. side, could not rely on any help from Liechtenstein, his *sole* state of nationality, since he did not have sufficient "genuine links" with that country.[133] This conclusion was reached notwithstanding the fact that he had purchased his nationality fully in line with the law of the principality and international law and did not have any other.[134] It is most ironical that the German authorities confirmed in a separate statement that Nottebohm was *not* a German citizen from the moment of naturalization in Liechtenstein. However "genuine" in the eyes of the court, legally speaking his links with Germany were nonexistent. The outcome of the case, which is undoubtedly one of the most misquoted in the corpus of international law,[135] continues to be criticized today, as it was with abundant clarity by the dissenting judges mainly for one great reason:[136] requiring "genuine links" pretends that citizenship is not an abstract legal status—a legal fiction—thus depriving anyone who happens to live a life and do business abroad of any diplomatic and consular protection even in a case of outright theft of all their property, as was the unfortunate experience of Nottebohm.

The good news is that *Nottebohm* is no longer considered good law, as Alice Sironi, among numerous others, has demonstrated with brilliance and clarity.[137] Indeed, the leading legal systems in the world have moved away from this dubious ideal of no legal protection based on a pretense that citizenship is not an abstract legal status, but rather something (vaguely) "genuine," as were the required "links" in *Nottebohm*. The case was rejected by numerous authorities worldwide—sometimes very explicitly, as in the European Union, for instance. The EU member states are prohibited by the European Court of Justice from failing to recognize one another's nationalities, which are soundly acquired under national law.[138] In the *Micheletti* case Spain tried to rely on the "genuine links" reasoning derived from *Nottebohm* to deny any rights to a dual Italian-Argentinian national who had never lived in Italy, by claiming that he was more Argentinian than Italian.[139] Giuseppe Tesauro, the outraged Italian Advocate General in this case has famously characterized *Nottebohm* as belonging to a "romantic period of international law,"[140] dismissing it outright, as did the European Court of Justice, opting instead for legal certainty and guaranteed protection of the rights of the migrant Europeans. The abstract nature of citizenship as a legal status has thus been defended and reaffirmed, as has the idea of due process of law. Indeed, following the "genuine links" logic would lock every citizen within the confines of the state of nationality, thus at times shrinking the whole world to a dot—think of Liechtenstein in the *Nottebohm* case. As international law and practice stands today, the key trend is to accord importance to the protection of rights and judicial review—the logic opposing the thinking underpinning *Nottebohm*. This is no surprise, since citizenship, as we have seen, is precisely based on an abstract equal connection to an authority claiming your person independently of your thoughts, talents, feelings, and actions. By definition it does *not* always correspond with the realities one might observe on the ground. Indeed, the status was created precisely to render those realities in many ways invisible from the outset.

The reasoning of the Court of Justice of the EU is even more valuable in light of the drastic difference in the quality of the statuses of nationality distributed around the world. The widely assumed mythology of the equality of different nationalities notwithstanding, if pushed to the extreme, the "genuine links" logic, which the European Court of Justice has discarded would require expatriates in less successful countries to naturalize where their "genuine links" are perceived to be in order to have a hope of protecting their property and rights, thereby acquiring deeply inferior, if not outright harmful, rightless nationalities—such as the Central African Republic's or Afghanistan's—something no minimally rational person can be expected to do, especially given that in the cases of a handful of nationalities still intolerant to the idea of citizenship cumulation, such legal confirmation of "genuine links" would amount to a loss of precious Austrian, German, Latvian, or Singaporean nationality. This has no doubt been the reason why Nottebohm, having lived his whole life in Guatemala and undoubtedly having "genuine links" with the Central American country, decided to naturalize in Liechtenstein, not there. This seems also to be the key distinction between expats—the holders of elite nationalities comfortable with the idea of returning to their well-governed and prosperous countries of origin—and migrants, the holders of undesirable second-rate citizenships. It is thus perfectly understandable that an Uzbek or a Ghanaian would normally never be referred to as an "expat," while a Swiss or a Canadian certainly would.

The core of *Nottebohm* reasoning is thus nothing but abstract moralizing, hypocrisy purified. As we have seen, the communities of citizens are not choice based. The sin committed by Nottebohm consisted in not accepting this sad reality: being a German who had spent his whole life in Guatemala and had probably not shared his compatriots' obsession with the *Führer*,[141] and who did not make secret of the fact that he had only naturalized in Liechtenstein in order to lose the status of a German and not take part in the hateful craze the Third Reich started. Instead of a demonstration of a clear anti-war and anti-totalitarian civic position, this was implicitly viewed by the International Court of Justice as an attempt to avoid responsibility for the war as a German. The Cold War-era court informed the world that in international law justice meant dispossession and exile based on guilt by association. Nottebohm did not start, support, or finance the war, only looking on from his distant Guatemalan home. In fact, his willful loss of German citizenship is the best indicator of what he thought about the politics of the Third Reich at the time.

The *Nottebohm*-style moralizing pushes citizenship's inescapable totalitarianism to extremes and for that reason would not fly in a contemporary legal context. Besides that, it is a necessary building block of citizenship as a legal status: all of us are judged by the color of our passport and nothing else at any international border. A Pakistani is bound to be "randomly" searched countless times and often denied admission. A red Norwegian passport—a super-élite brother of the Swiss, the Singaporean, and the Monegasque—on the contrary, will let the holder in with a nod and a smile. Guilt by association is undoubtedly an essential starting point of citizenship.

As a result of more than 170 in absentia proceedings of different kinds in Guatemalan courts, Guatemala seized a fortune of almost seven million Swiss francs from Nottebohm—which would be infinitely more, of course, in contemporary value. The ICJ refused to allow Liechtenstein to contest this, while underlining that "it is up to Liechtenstein, as it is for every sovereign State, to settle by its own legislation the rules relating to the acquisition of its nationality [...] it is not necessary to determine whether international law imposes any limitation on its freedom of decision in this domain."[142] This did not prevent the judges, voting 11 to 3, from allowing Guatemala to rob Friedrich Nottebohm of his possessions while prohibiting his only state of nationality from defending him. So much for international law.

The "instrument and object of closure"[143] is quite dynamic in essence, as this overview demonstrates. The core of citizenship is always there and there are no signs of it going away, however: it is a status of random and absolute subjugation to a public authority, with nothing to do with the identity, choice, or desire of the holder. Based on the fictions of unalienable dignity and equality between all the communities of citizens around the world, the status of citizenship has traditionally performed its functions of reinforcing inequalities, combined with sexist and racial subjugation and the humiliation of the dissenters and minorities, while deploying the language of equality, dignity, and destiny. As the racist and anti-egalitarian core of the status becomes ever more pronounced when one looks at how it works between states, within one state, the status is becoming less racist, sexist, and intolerant, amenable to cumulation and re- ethnicization as well as de-ethnicization. In so becoming, citizenship potentially debunks its very core, which is the justification for the systemic, randomized subjugation of the "other" while ensuring smooth governability of a narrow selection of those who are proclaimed to belong. The status is thus becoming less and less effective in performing its function of facilitating sexist, racist, and economic subjugation within states, while still effectively cutting the legal boundaries of exclusion between and through societies. The most important lesson that emerges, however, is that citizenship cannot by definition have any dignity of its own. Those who claim this to be the case are blind to the ethical void underpinning its distribution, and the effectiveness of its servile nature in helping justify oppression and humiliation throughout its history.

RIGHTS

Those who hold the status of citizen are entitled to citizenship rights based on that status. The most important rights, this chapter argues, are those allowing citizens to enter the territory controlled by the authority issuing the status and to reside and work there, without a threat of being deported abroad. However obvious this might sound, the story in the majority of textbooks is quite different, astonishingly. I will explain why the textbooks take a wrong approach. British sociologist T. H. Marshall is the key reference on this. In his popular lecture delivered at Cambridge in 1949, Marshall, using his native England as a case study, outlined three generations of citizenship rights, attempting to trace the path of citizenship. The account he gave is still immensely popular with sociologists, political scientists, and philosophers of citizenship today. Approaching citizenship rights chronologically, Marshall identified civil, political, and social rights, emerging in succession and corresponding roughly to the ideas on citizenship in the eighteenth, nineteenth, and twentieth centuries. Civil rights include *habeas corpus* liberty of the person, and freedom of religion, speech, and thought. Political rights relate to participation in the exercise of political power. Social rights are about social welfare and security.

The core explicit lesson one draws from T. H. Marshall's writings is about the important role that citizenship rights played in supplying "the foundations of equality on which the structures of inequality could be built."[1] Citizenship thus emerges as a key tool for the preservation of social inequality and deeply stratified class structures: while civil rights ensured a successful transition from a status of feudal attachment to the ability to enter contracts freely, making the labor force freely available on the market, social rights relieved the industry of social responsibility beyond the labor contract.[2] Broadened political rights socialized the "minimal human being," in John Mueller's words, into the mythology of equality and self-government, as we will discuss in more detail in chapter 5. This happened on the premise that it is elections, more than anything else, that affect the business of government. Writes Mueller: "It is true that each member of the electorate in modern democracies has more or less the same voting strength at the ballot box. However ... the political importance of an individual is not very significantly determined by this circumstance, and therefore political inequality effectively prospers: some people are, in fact, more equal than others. A store clerk has the same weight in an election as the head of a big corporation or a columnist for the *Washington Post*, but it would be absurd to suggest they are remotely equal in their ability to affect and influence government policy."[3]

There is a potentially more important lesson to draw from T. H. Marshall's writings, however, and this one is implicit: the deep-rooted complacency lying at the core of scholarly thinking about citizenship. Marshall does not question the status at all. The citizenship he works with is a "status bestowed on those who are full members of a community."[4] Just as the absolute majority of citizens have always been taught to do, he takes for granted what authority decides: those who are not citizens—and are not granted rights—are thus "not members," full stop. In his world, composed of one country/one society/one body of citizens, all the most important contradictions of citizenship status, which we analyzed in chapter 2, manage to remain entirely hidden, as Marshall's iconic definition denies the constitutive nature of the status of citizenship. As a result, he, along with his countless followers, missed citizenship's essential function, which is exclusion on the grounds of mere status assignment. This brings with it, as we saw in the previous chapter, legal erasure based on any grounds, particularly race and sex, while invoking dignity and equality as rationales for these ugly outcomes, something fully accepted by the majority of those who have already acquired the status. Marshall's citizenship and equality story, although posing, oxymoronically, as universally English, is thus applicable for certain solely to the likes of himself—white gentlemen with a solid immigration status in the UK and a solid income, teaching at the London School of Economics, as he did. However much respect such citizens deserve, the omission of all other people, the majority, looms: for them the most crucial citizenship rights disappear, including the right to enter the state territory and remain as long as they want free of border controls, to work, and to not be deported. These rights are of no relevance for those who pretend that the whole world is one country. Such pretense is vital to see citizenship as just.

Worse still: in the case of T. H. Marshall's England, what he failed to notice was not only the world abroad, but also the rest of the Empire (not necessarily "foreign lands" strictly speaking). This England-centered account dismisses all legally inferior subjects who are not in the territory of the British Isles proper and who enjoy no rights because of gender, skin color, and other equally inequitable considerations. In one of the best criticisms of Marshallian legal obscurantism, Luigi Ferrajoli has demonstrated that Marshall's questionable fundamental assumption—that of course brown colonials under the same monarch and with the same passport "do not belong" and are not "full members of the community"—is symptomatic of the poverty of numerous sociological accounts of citizenship failing to approach the notion sufficiently critically.[5] Worse still, such a complacent approach also leads to deep misrepresentations of the essence of what amounts to citizenship rights, as will be discussed. This concerns, in particular, the importance of the notion of territory in the context of the construction of rights.

Rights and Boundaries

By being essentially territorial through its inherent connection to a state (which is by definition a territorial entity), citizenship, no matter how it is acquired, limits our spatial imagination: it sets the boundaries of our world, teaching every good citizen to think in terms of the "natural" limitations that the immigration borders of the state conferring the status erects. The litmus test of this is the visualization of the weather forecast on your smartphone, commuter train, or in your elevator: suns and clouds crowd together to form a shape, roughly, of the country you supposedly inhabit. The weather in a city next door to you will be off limits if that city is "foreign." All spheres of human existence are affected by this territoriality, not only the anticipation of the sun and rain. This is the paradigm of the limitations on everyone's physical horizon of opportunities, which we are taught to accept from primary school—not only the Argentine children, whose exciting pledge we saw. It is reinforced by the second boundary the state polices: the boundary of the body of citizenry, which follows the status distribution rules and usually cuts right through any society. The most dramatic point about focusing on the rights of citizenship as T. H. Marshall defined them is that you must choose not to notice the plight of those, many of them de facto or even de jure citizens, who fall within at least two important categories. The first are those who do not get any access to the territory and hence, no rights guaranteed in it. The second are those who do not have access to the status of citizenship in law or in fact, while being part of society.

To provide a full account of citizenship's essence, the rights that relate to access to and presence in the territory of the authority granting the status are what lay the foundations for the enjoyment of any other rights. The most important rights of citizenship are thus the right to enter, the right to remain in and be economically active in the territory, and the right to not be deported to any area where the suns and the clouds are not displayed. These obviously interrelated rights are dissected into several categories in the majority of the legal systems around the globe. Entering a country on a tourist visa or a visa waiver does not usually mean that you can be gainfully employed, and once a work permit is granted, it usually will not be of unlimited duration: permanent settlement is not implied, requiring—if you are not a citizen and thus do not possess an automatic right—a totally different kind of documentation: a long-term residence permit, a green card, an indefinite leave to remain. Passport stamps, the constant pressure put on the airlines and ferry companies, which become the decentralized agents of enforcement of strict immigration regimes, coupled with modern IT border-crossing and international information exchange systems help states check and enforce compliance with the three degrees of the right to be present in the territory outlined above, forming three levels of inclusion.

The inequalities these three levels of inclusion (temporary visitor status, permanent resident status, citizenship status) generate are difficult to appreciate from the vantage point of a holder of an elite citizenship. Already speaking about the most basic freedom—freedom of travel—the world could roughly be divided, following Yossi Harpaz's suggestion, into three categories of citizenships: the top-tier citizenships allowing temporary visa-free access to the EU (Schengen territory, comprising the majority of EU member states, as well as Iceland, Norway, Switzerland, and all of Europe's microstates) and the United States; second-tier nationalities granting only Schengen territory access, and all the other statuses, whose holders are unable even to travel without preauthorizations, let alone to live or work in the most affluent countries as of right, without any need for permits and visas (see figure 5). This division of the world showcases the complete exclusion of the former colonies and the majority of the former socialist countries with the exception of the ones that made it into the EU from the global geography of mobility rights. The overwhelming rights to travel without any pre-clearances, which only the holders of the most elite nationalities receive, create an illusion of an open and welcoming world among the holders of the world's elite super-citizenships. The same world emerges in an overwhelmingly different light for the holders of third-tier statuses—Indians, Russians, the Chinese—who are only welcome to visit a few of the former colonies of the most highly developed states visa free. The discriminatory assumptions underpinning the system are sometimes actually written into your document after the visit. When you enter the island of Curaçao, an officer will stamp your passport with "*No es permitido trabajar.*" As you leave, the language, and the message too, change to "Thank you for visiting our beautiful island." Latin American migrants—who are presumed to be planning to overstay their welcome—are warned in their own mother tongue, while the American yachtsmen are thanked—which is also polite.[6] In fact, the message in Spanish is not even applicable to the majority of Americans: through a bilateral agreement, U.S. citizens are free to stay in the Dutch overseas possessions as long as they wish and can also work if they like.[7]

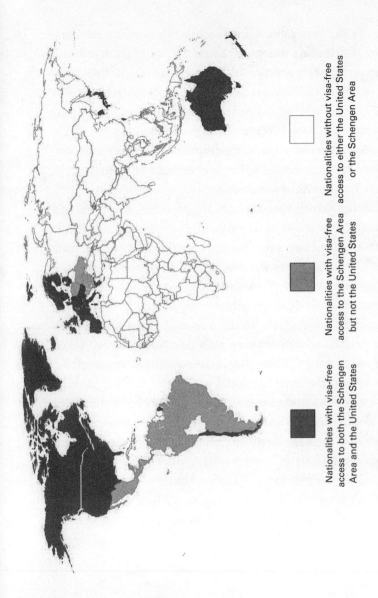

Figure 5 Nationalities of the world by visa-free tourist access to the United States and the Schengen Area

Source: Y. Harpaz, "North vs. South, or Integrated vs. Isolated? Notes on the Global Grouping of Nationalities," in *Kälin and Kochenov's Quality of Nationality Index,* ed. D. Kochenov and J. Lindeboom (Oxford: Hart Publishing, 2019).

As the core right of citizenship is accessing the territory of the state granting the status for any duration of stay and for all purposes, all other rights necessarily come later, especially political, social, and civil rights. These can only be the starting point for analysis if access to the territory is presumed. Yet, such an assumption is untenable in a world where thousands die every year trying to penetrate militarized and sealed borders. Historically, the approach to territory was different of course: as John Torpey observes, "Until the ultimate triumph of capitalism and the nation-state in nineteenth-century Europe … controls on movement remained predominantly an "internal" matter."[8] State territory was not unbroken in the eyes of the citizens back then: the abolition of internal frontiers was viewed as one of the key achievements of the modernizing wave of the French Revolution. Also outside France, until the mid-twentieth century a Californian could be jailed for six months for bringing an unemployed brother from Texas into the state, as states saw it as one of their vital tasks to protect the local population from the presence of poor Americans coming from elsewhere in the country.[9] This was the case until the Supreme Court struck down such limitations in 1941 in the name of the freedom of travel as a right of national citizenship implied in the U.S. Constitution.[10] The European Union has followed suit by turning the freedom of movement of its citizens into a sacred cow of its legal system,[11] and the post-Soviet countries abolished their *propiska* regimes, which used to negate for the citizens the internal unity of the territory of the USSR.[12] Until very recently China remained the main major nation that continued to deny its citizens the ability to choose where to live within the country, preserving inequality in society by using geography to imprison the majority of the rural populations socially, politically, and economically. Interestingly, legal prohibitions on movement have almost never in human history been fully effective, as proven by 300 million Chinese internal migrants and countless Soviet peasants before them,[13] who found their way into the cities in search of minimal freedom and prosperity, providing living examples of the limited nature of the law's claim to authority.

The simple and straightforward hierarchy between access to territory and all the other rights is not at all a reflection of a random preference: removal from the territory can be a tool of deprivation of rights as effective as the deprivation of the status of citizenship as such. Pushing dissenters beyond the territorial boundary or the boundary of citizenship are among the best-tested strategies for depriving someone of political influence and uprooting a life. Examples of this abound from Themistocles in Argos, to Aleksander Herzen scribbling in London,[14] and Kaiser Wilhelm chopping wood in Doorn.[15] In a move against freedom, even in music, the Brazilian junta imprisoned and exiled in 1968 both leaders of the Tropicália movement.[16] The grounds for driving them out included Caetano Veloso and Gilberto Gil disobeying the ban on playing electric guitars. Citizenship boundaries exclude even more effectively, potentially disqualifying individuals from politics *and* prohibiting reentry. Mikheil Saakashvili, the former Georgian president, who was invited by President Poroshenko to help put Ukraine back on track in 2015 after the Russia-instigated hostilities and the loss of Crimea, was deprived of Ukrainian citizenship in 2017 in a move to preempt his political ambitions and silence his criticism of the corrupt administration of the sitting president.[17] Leon Trotsky, deprived of citizenship, sent into exile, and ultimately killed by Stalin, is an example of a rebel pushed beyond all three boundaries: territory, citizenship, and life itself.[18] Exile as the harshest form of punishment predates contemporary citizenship, of course: Socrates famously chose death over it.

The Arendtian characterization of citizenship as a "right to have rights"[19] does not concern merely citizenship as a status—it is a citizenship with the right to enter and stay in the territory of the state granting it. The vast majority of citizenships around the world come with an unquestionable right to enter the state that granted your citizenship.[20] A passport attesting to your citizenship status sends one crucial signal to all the governments in the world: the state mentioned on the cover is where you can be deported to, should any problems arise. "At home," numerous states around the world even guarantee that criminal citizens will not be extradited. This includes mass murderers, such as several Croatian generals who only ended up in the hands of the International Criminal Tribunal for the Former Yugoslavia in The Hague after overwhelming pressure from the European Union[21] and in contradiction to numerous pledges of President Tuđman to not extradite the genocidal torturers who were "simply defending the country."[22] The right to remain in the territory of your state of nationality is thus *the* citizenship right, making the majority of other rights possible in a situation where the whole world territory is divided between states. Indeed, it can be argued that it is probably the only "absolute" citizenship right that legal or illegal residents, however permanent, who do not possess a citizenship status do not enjoy.[23]

In the states' world the situation of non-citizens is precarious by definition, no matter what kind of visas and permits they hold: only the status of citizenship of the state of residence protects the life lived in a particular state or territory. It is easy to have your life shattered if you are not a citizen of the place where you live, thus not enjoying the unconditional right to stay. On numerous occasions, a simple policy change, as opposed to any behavior frowned upon by the state of residence—smoking pot in Germany, stamping on money with the portrait of the local King in Thailand, taking a selfie with naked buttocks on top of a Malaysian mountain, signing a check that bounces in Dubai, or bathing topless in Kuwait—can get you deported, often overriding the promise of permanence behind your immigration status, which you as a non-citizen happen to hold. Offending local sensibilities by pulling moonies or smoking pot is not necessary, however. The DACA kids did nothing wrong; similarly the best-paid and educated foreigners in Australia were completely law abiding, when the government simply decided in 2017 to abolish a whole class of visas for educated people "Type 457"—potentially turning Australia into a difficult place for the most qualified.[24] When policy changes are in sight, it is foreignness as such that is the guarantor of differentiated treatment. Citizenship protects against deportation caused by either one's own behavior or by policy claustrophobia, or both. Once again: your foreignness has nothing to do with your habits, education, religion, or linguistic skills—it is a purely legal category, as we have seen in chapter 2. Consequently, only the status of local citizenship ensures permanence in the territory. Regrettably for many, acquiring such a status will often not be an option and the considerations behind granting it will be as random as they are at times unreasonable: an Estonian great grandfather could be more helpful than living your whole life in and being born in Estonia. Similarly, policy changes can concern the boundaries of citizenry as such, producing countless foreigners overnight, as occurred in Nazi Germany, apartheid South Africa, newly independent Slovenia, contemporary India, or the Dominican Republic—among countless other places—and will no doubt happen again countless times as long as citizenship exists.

The Decoupling of Territory and Citizenship

It is difficult to present the prevailing status quo as just, of course. It is thus unsurprising that the world is slowly moving away from the strict correlation between the status of citizenship and the corresponding territory of rights. Two trends in citizenship development around the world affect the correlation between possessing the status of citizenship and the crucial citizenship right to stay in the territory. The first protects non-citizens through appeals to human rights, thus producing de facto citizens, enjoying the core citizenship right of unlimited access to territory without however benefiting from the formal legal status; the second extends the territory of rights beyond the territory of the state that granted you citizenship. Both trends are fundamental for understanding contemporary citizenship.

The European continental system of human rights protection is at the forefront of the first trend, which in essence means one thing: the gradual evaporation of the abstract character of the status of citizenship, making the policing of the citizen/non-citizen boundaries that cut across European societies increasingly difficult day by day—a welcome development, should we take issue with the exclusion citizenship brings. The most interesting examples of this come from the case law of the European Court of Human Rights, which is charged with policing the observance of the European Convention on Human Rights, currently ratified by forty-seven European states from Ireland to Russia, Sweden to Azerbaijan. Under established legal practice, state parties to the Convention cannot deport foreigners who have built essential ties with the society where they reside. Only the actual life as lived counts, the formal criterion of the legality of presence is often of no relevance to the Court. Among the first cases starting this trend was *Beldjoudi v. France*,[25] where France was prohibited from deporting an Algerian criminal who had never been to Algeria, having been born in France and failing to register as French following Algerian secession from France in 1962. Mohand Beldjoudi spent one third of his life in French jails, serving five sentences of a total duration of almost eight years by the time the case was decided. The European Court of Human Rights found that the ties between the criminal and French society were too strong to cut on the basis merely of the fact that Beldjoudi did not possess the status of citizenship and was supposed to have been deported from the country according to the

French authorities. Judge Martens, in his famous concurring opinion in the case, concluded that "mere nationality does not constitute an objective and reasonable justification for the existence of a difference as regards the admissibility of expelling someone from what ... may be called his 'own country.'"[26] The UN Human Rights Committee arrived at a similar conclusion, advising Canada not to remove a Brit brought to Canada at the age of seven for whom Canada had become his "own country," although he had never naturalized.[27]

Among the latest examples of this line of case law in Europe is *Jeunesse v. Netherlands*, where the Netherlands was prohibited from deporting to Suriname the illegally present wife of a Dutchman and mother of three Dutch-national kids. Although "illegal," Meriam Jeunesse used to be Dutch, since she was born before Suriname became an independent country.[28] A heavy blow is being struck at the abstractness of citizenship status as well as at state policy choices for dealing with perceived illegal residents.[29] What this case law reveals is that the main beneficiary of rights is not the figure of a citizen in possession of formal legal status of equality to other citizens, but a human being, with a life of work, love and relationships, from marriage to friendships. Clearly, deporting the DACA kids from the United States would have been outright impossible under the continent-wide European rules. Yet many of the de facto citizens benefiting the most from the European

Court of Human Rights' approach creating a de facto nationality, are actually born in Europe, meaning that in the United States, with its *ius soli*, they would have been natural-born Americans rather than illegal immigrants, thus enjoying an absolute right to reside in U.S. territory. The two systems, demonstrating radically different approaches to solving the conundrums of citizenship and legal residence are thus just and unjust in almost complementary ways. The European approach is not without a strange twist: solitary people without family networks and friends would most likely not benefit from protection against deportation from home, since the legal basis used is "family life."

The distribution of citizenship status as such is not prone to being subjected to human rights-based limitations. In terms of the actual citizenship held, Beldjoudi remains Algerian in the eyes of French law, just as Jeunesse is Surinamese in the Netherlands. By disconnecting the formal status of citizenship from the most deeply cherished and crucial right this status brings, European human rights protection law has taken the side of concrete human beings as opposed to abstract citizens. The possession of an abstract legal status is no longer indispensable to the enjoyment of the core citizenship right to remain.

The second trend in the development of the right of access to a territory of citizenship is equally far-reaching. The citizenship status issued by many nations around the world is no longer limited to the territory controlled by the issuing authority. The majority of the citizenships of the most highly developed nations are passports to full inclusion in dozens of states, rather than to one state only. This alters a crucial aspect of the rights story: the rights' scope. Almost half the nations around the world today issue citizenship statuses recognized by other nations, in terms of often virtually unconditional access to national territory for work and settlement. So, a Bahraini is welcome in the other five Gulf Cooperation Council states,[30] a Norwegian in forty-one European nations, and an Armenian in Belarus, Georgia, Kazakhstan, and Kyrgyzstan[31] and in the Russian Federation. From ECOWAS in Western Africa,[32] OECS in the Caribbean,[33] and MERCOSUR in Latin America[34] to the Trans-Tasman Travel Agreement of 1973 between New Zealand and Australia and the core rights granted to Indians in Nepal and Bhutan, as well as the full access to the U.S. territory and labor market granted to Nauru, Palau, and FS Micronesia citizens,[35] the decoupling of the territory where the core nonpolitical rights of citizenship are enjoyed and the territory of the state granting citizenship is now a universal phenomenon.

While seemingly revolutionary, such interpenetration of territorial rights was anticipated by the legendary English constitutionalist Albert Venn Dicey as long ago as 1897. Addressing the Fellows of All Souls at Oxford, Dicey put forward a proposal for Anglo-Saxon "intercitizenship":

full mutual recognition of citizenships between the British Empire and the United States, to mark the coming of the twentieth century.[36] Although not taken seriously at that time, Dicey actually predicted the future: whether we like it or not, the separation of the world into states and of the people of the world into citizens is arbitrary. States with similar cultures and close ties between populations were bound to correct the steep arbitrary exclusions created by the legal proclamation of foreignness affecting their populations. Intercitizenships proposed by Dicey are thus one of the core elements of the citizenship landscape in the twenty-first-century world, shaping the rights enjoyed by hundreds of millions of individuals around the globe. In the current context, as the map in figure 6 demonstrates, it is more atypical than not to have a strict correlation between state citizenship and territory in terms of the geographical scope of the rights of residence and work that the citizens would enjoy. Countries such as Sri Lanka, Namibia, or China, whose citizens do not enjoy rights to settle and work anywhere in the world outside their national territory (or, in the case of China, merely a part of national territory, Hong Kong and Macao lying behind a visa wall even for tourist travel for the majority of the Chinese citizens) have come to be an exception, even though the monolithic citizenship/state-territory correlation they espouse would have generally been the rule around the world only a hundred years ago, albeit a different world, if we

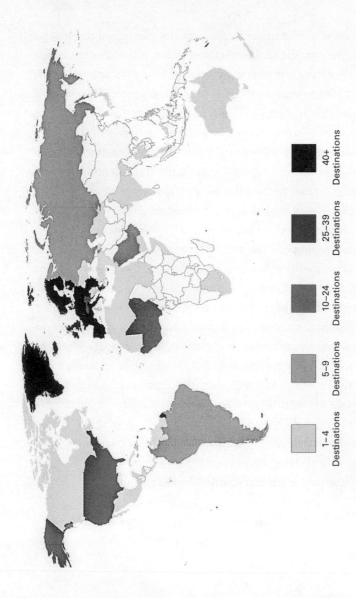

Figure 6 Intercitizenships of the world
Source: Author's original research. The dataset is also used in the QNI methodology, www.nationalityindex.com.

consider all the differences between the world of empires and the current world of states.

This change can be explained by two triggers. The first is the emergence of regional integration blocks (EU, MERCOSUR, OECS, ECOWAS) unwilling to allow—along the lines of thinking in Judge Martens's concurring opinion in *Beldjoudi v. France*—the unjustified exclusion based merely on the "foreigner" legal status. The second trigger is the gradual deterioration of the former empires with continuing postcolonial ties, as attested to by the gradually waning intercitizenships of the former Soviet space and between some parts of the former British Empire (India and its satellites, Australia and New Zealand) as well as the U.S. empire (states in free association). An intermediary option fusing both lines of developments is also possible, as demonstrated by the Latin American countries enjoying historical colonial ties and a peculiarly open approach to territorial rights attaching to their citizenships, as well as revamped integration in the sphere of migration— mostly via MERCOSUR—as Diego Acosta Arcarazo has demonstrated.[37]

Key Citizenship Rights and Discrimination

The preceding two trends aside, the territorial operation of citizenship rights has at times been marred by contradictions. To state simply that citizenship always comes with the right to enter, work, and remain in a territory is to conceal citizenship's racist or sexist face: the Devil is, as always, in the detail. In the course of history states have always been disconnecting the citizenship held by particular groups from its core rights, including the most important: residence. The UK easily provides the most telling examples of the harshness of such chronic discrimination. To take race as an example, decolonization resulted in whole groups of British citizens being trapped between different forms of racism. Upon the proclamation of independence, the East African rulers in Tanganyika, Kenya, and Uganda introduced racist citizenship laws— some of them still in place[38]—and a policy of "Africanization," turning 200,000 British citizens, mostly of Indian descent, into refugees. Not black enough to be citizens of where they had been born and resided, they remained solely the citizens of the UK and—deprived by the new African states of both citizenship status and the most basic protections of rights—they faced race-based expulsions and an extreme deterioration of their socioeconomic status. Escaping to the UK would have been the refugees' only route to safety had Her Majesty's government not introduced racist restrictions on these citizens' entry and residence, while leaving citizenship laws intact. Some full British citizens were thus not only not black enough, but equally not white enough to enjoy key rights.[39]

During three days of 1968, at the height of the East African Asian crisis, with more than six thousand British citizen refugees arriving per month, the Wilson government passed emergency legislation decoupling UK citizenship—quite astonishingly—from the right to enter the UK. All British citizens unable to trace their ancestry to a parent or a grandparent born or naturalized on the British Isles lost the right to enter their own country. In the words of Anthony, Lord Lester of Herne Hill, who was involved in fighting the legislation in the international courts, "a group of British citizens, temporary in public office, successfully used their legislative majority to abridge the basic rights and freedoms of another group of British citizens, because of their colour and ethnic origins."[40] An impenetrable newly erected immigration boundary cutting through the body of full UK citizens was indeed solely based on race and was in direct opposition to the "sovereign citizen" approach embraced by the U.S. Supreme Court as we have seen in chapter 2. Only the white British citizens were sovereign and secure in their rights and status possession.[41] The origins of "European-looking" Britons would not be checked at all.[42] Left in suspense, with British passports in hand, as beautiful as they were unusable, the British East African Asian community, deprived of all rights, experienced total devastation. Countless heartbreaking stories of British citizens sent back to the brutal post-colonial dictatorships from their only country of citizenship—the UK—are reported. The Home Secretary's memorandum, never mentioning race, spoke of a group of "citizens of the UK ... who have no substantial connection to this country."[43] The UK, even having lost a high-profile court case at the Council of Europe refused to change this racist practice, depriving "non-patrial" citizens of the absolute majority of their rights by denying them access to the UK. The Commission on Human Rights of the Council of Europe considered it "established that the 1968 Act had racial motives and that it covered a racial group. When it was introduced into parliament as a bill, it was clear that it was directed against the Asian citizens of the United Kingdom and Colonies in East Africa and especially those in Kenya."[44]

To say that the UK learned from the crisis would probably be excessive, as Olivier Bancoult, the leader of the exiled Chagossian community told me while treating me to a meal of goat, Chagos-style, in his headquarters on Mauritius. Chagossians were kicked out of their archipelago in the beginning of the 1970s by the British military only to learn later that their islands had always been "uninhabited" by law and thus fit for lease to the United States to build there the largest U.S. naval base abroad.[45] The House of Lords has eagerly confirmed the legality of the UK's actions under the greatest of the unwritten constitutions. As explained by Lord Hoffmann, "The right of abode is a creature of the law. The law gives it and the law may take it away. In this context I do not think that it assists the argument to call it a constitutional right."[46] Chagossians can now enter the UK on their UK passports, but Diego Garcia, the main island, just like the rest of the Chagos Archipelago, is closed to them: the settlement in the "uninhabited" British Indian Ocean Territory is expressly prohibited by the Constitution of the Territory—an act of the UK executive in the writing of which the Chagossians did not take any part.[47] The traditions of the islands live on in a community-owned high-rise at the outskirts of London and at a tiny cultural center on Mauritius. Many more examples of groups holding citizenships without core rights can be provided, the United States supplying the latest one by confiscating the passports of Yemeni Americans in Sana'a, de facto denying its own citizens access to national territory, effectively depriving them of a route to escape a war zone.[48] It is thus possible even today to hold the citizenship of a powerful democracy and essentially not to enjoy any rights through the operation of law based on ethnic origin: the traditions set by the UK are alive and well in its former colonies.

This has to be restated: notwithstanding the fact that official accounts would usually tell a different tale, many states are fine-tuned to keep their citizens down, purposefully excluding specific groups, not infrequently majorities, either under the pretext of not extending full status of citizenship or limiting essential rights.[49] This is usually done in the name of equality, the core dignitarian citizenship trump card: all *patrials* should be equal: how can non-patrial citizens be allowed to have any rights in the UK? The stories of the Chagossians and the East African Asians as well as U.S. Yemenis today are just a drop in an ocean of such examples. British Overseas Territories Citizenship status issued by the UK still does not grant its owners the automatic right to settle and work anywhere per se.[50] British Subject status, still held by a handful of former British Imperial Subjects—does not even permit them to visit the UK without applying for a tourist visa. The people brought down by their nations almost invariably belong to specific ethnic groups, showcasing the biases at play behind the neat beauty of citizenship's façade. Ethnic discrimination is thus key to understanding the meaning and functions of citizenship.

Citizenship can be useless in practice, however, even if your rights are safeguarded on paper. To see this, imagine you are a citizen of Abkhazia on the Black Sea, the Sahrawi Republic in Western Sahara, or Somaliland, which despite managing to set the limit of your horizon of opportunities vis-à-vis the rest of the world, do not exist at all as far as international lawyers are concerned: unrecognized states are the outlaws of the world community, and whatever legal statuses they ascribe to their populations cannot officially matter outside their borders.[51] Being an international outcast of a noncountry is not necessary to make a questionable citizenship status. The best examples are provided by any country in disarray, such as Afghanistan, Libya, or Syria. Possessing the citizenship of such places cannot but point in one direction: you are de facto stateless and should not expect too many rights from the unfortunate outcome of the birthright lottery in your particular case. To make matters worse, being de facto stateless is not the same as not having any citizenship at all. As a citizen of Libya you will not even benefit from any additional protections offered to people who are actually stateless, such as shorter qualification periods for naturalization elsewhere or the automatic acquisition of the citizenship of the European country of birth by your children.[52] De facto protection from deportation, which stateless persons unwanted anywhere enjoy will not apply either. You will therefore father or give birth to a Libyan child and can be deported to Libya from anywhere you happen to settle even though your citizenship, coming with an attractive right to enter a war zone at any time, is a liability rather than a boon.

Directly mirroring the right to remain is the right to leave. Although codified in international law, it is often ephemeral in practice. This was particularly true during the Cold War, when the Soviet camp—including pretty much all the satellite states under Soviet control—as well as some nonaligned countries fearing the mythical brain drain, were de facto turned into a huge prison, while unable to offer proper opportunities to their own citizens, no matter how well-intentioned or educated.[53] Those escaping were condemned by the state, for *a good citizen does not leave*—even if the country is a disaster and the citizenship it provides does more harm than good. While generally respected nowadays, the right to leave a country is not recognized by a handful of nations preserving the Soviet approach to rights and freedoms, such as Turkmenistan, North Korea, Cuba, and a handful of other dictatorships.

The Decoupling of Citizenship and Rights

The core citizenship rights related to access to the territory are indispensable for the enjoyment of the other citizenship rights: civil, social, and political. Strangely, as with Marshall, access to territory rights often tend to be invisible in the literature on citizenship, as opposed to migration literature, due to the former's tendency to pretend that all the countries—political communities—exist in a vacuum, as we have seen in chapter 2. Ironically, moving beyond the unconditional right to enter, remain, and work in the territory of a state—in other words, precisely before we enter the territory of so-called classical Marshall's rights—citizenship rights in the strict sense tend to end. What Marshall described in terms of civil, social, and political citizenship rights was probably correct for some jurisdictions at the time. Those holding the full status of belonging and finding themselves in the territory of the UK enjoyed habeas corpus, access to pensions and healthcare, and the right to vote. It did not reflect the full picture at all, however, because no citizenship of the UK and colonies was actually required for the enjoyment of most of these rights. We see this much better now. The triumph of the human rights ideology of the second half of the twentieth century brought with it a new emphasis: it is one's humanity rather than citizenship status that grants access to the majority of rights Marshall used to associate with that status.[54] Indeed, civil rights are part of the world's universal human rights heritage and social rights apply, without discrimination, to citizens and settled foreigners—usually those enjoying permanent residency status. Yasemin Soysal has famously characterized this shift as a move toward "post-national" citizenship.[55] This story, echoing Marshall's intuitions with which we started this chapter, is not necessarily anywhere near correct empirically, of course. Luigi Ferrajoli has successfully demonstrated the historical connections between what sociologists usually brand as "civil" and "social" rights and general personhood.[56] In fact, most embarrassingly for some, the distinction between citizenship and simple personhood in the context of these rights, besides famously flowing from the French *Declaration des droits de l'homme et du citoyen* of August 26, 1789,[57] was also set in stone in the Napoleonic Code, and the overwhelmingly powerful tradition it has initiated in legal practice and legal scholarship, allowing us to qualify both Marshallian intuitions and Soysal's revelations. Indeed, since almost time immemorial, "l'exercice des droits civils est independent de la qualité de citoyen."[58] What is left to citizenship, then, is unquestionable access to territory and to political rights—a tandem, which Marshall failed to grasp.

The connection between the status of citizenship and what Marshall termed as civil and social rights therefore is much less straightforward than sociologists and political scientists would assume. Given that citizenship status is crucial in terms of forging unconditional access to a territory where all these categories of rights take shape in the first place, a more faithful account would simply be to remove these rights from the palette of colors citizenship wields. These are no longer perceived, rightly, as uniquely citizenship rights, and inventing a new meaning for citizenship that would necessarily fail to capture the essence of the exclusionary status at its core is not necessarily helpful.

Being open about the shift of focus from citizenship rights to human rights is the core development in the context of the understanding of the nature of rights in the contemporary legal-political context. Christian Joppke refers to this trend as the "thinning of citizenship."[59] Formerly taken as a guarantor of crucial rights, the legal status of citizenship as understood today in fact shares its pedestal with permanent residence or sometimes simply person-hood as such. In other words, the importance of citizenship as a trigger for rights has unquestionably diminished in our understanding compared with a mere half century ago, since the status of citizenship issued by the authority in charge instead of holding the monopoly of Marshallian rights activation has no direct connection to the majority of such rights beyond providing the "entry card" to the territory where they play out, supplying the core rights related to unquestionable and unlimited presence and work in the territory. The growth of human rights, coupled with the critical scrutiny by the likes of Linda Bosniak, Luigi Ferrajoli, and Christian Joppke of the presumptions about the scope of each particular right entertained by T. H. Marshall and his followers has had a fundamental impact on our understanding of the meaning and scope of citizenship rights in the absolute majority of states.

Citizenship rights came to be strongly contested with the belief that humans as such—as opposed to merely certain groups of humans singled out based on the random assignment of abstract citizenship statuses—should be the beneficiaries of rights. Scholars finally read the Napoleonic Code. We have seen that no society is perfectly co-extensive with the group of the holders of citizenship of the country in question. Consequently, any right granted to citizens only, as opposed to all the permanent or other residents, or simply everyone who happens to be in the territory controlled by the responsible authority, conflicts with the idea of human rights as a general feature pertaining to all humans. The impact of this very clear and straightforward thinking on the essential content and functioning of citizenship rights has been stunning: all the core civil rights and the majority of social rights—from acquiring property and inheriting land to nondiscrimination in terms of pay, equal protection under the law, and entitlements to old-age pensions and social housing and assistance, where provided—are now extended based on some other criteria, usually the length of legal residence, rather than the status of citizenship as such.

All the core rights outlined by Marshall as the civil rights of citizenship thus have little to do with this status and belong to everyone who lives in or happens to visit a state territory. Once again: while this is a revelation for the sociologists, Ferrajoli is correct pointing out that, popular citizenship rights accounts notwithstanding, this has *always* been the case. The distinction between *status civitatis* (citizenship) and *status personae* (personhood in law) is one of the basics of legal studies.[60] The situation with social rights is very similar: all the Marshallian social rights usually extend to citizens and permanent residents.[61] The dynamics are different on the political side of the citizenship rights' spectrum, as will be discussed in chapter 5. The most important exception from this truly glorious march to rebrand citizenship rights as human rights over the last decades is the right to enter, work, and reside in a territory unconditionally. Not surprisingly, one would say, since this is precisely *not* a human right under the currently dominant understanding of the concept. The human rights ideology endorses and reinforces the compartmentalization of the territory of the world despite the obvious lack of ethical foundations to underpin this reality as Joseph Carens, inter alia, has brilliantly argued.[62] At the same time, since the absolute majority of all the relevant rights outlined are undoubtedly territorial, the right to enter, work, and reside, although purely a citizenship right, is unquestionably of fundamental importance in the context of benefiting from all the other rights too.

The proud place of the abstract legal status of citizenship as the main trigger of rights has thus been seriously challenged. One of the key reasons behind this Joppkian thinning of citizenship lies at the core of the status: its arbitrary nature fits uneasily within the modern legal world where authorities must give reasons and the ideals of rationality and merit come to the fore in the context of the shift from what Moshe Cohen-Eliya and Iddo Porat describe as the "culture of authority" to the "culture of justification."[63] The public now demands to be convinced, as opposed to being dictated to. The choices made by public authorities must thus be justified in an officially declared open war on randomness and arbitrariness. Citizenship, as a uniquely arbitrary status, has systemic difficulties in this context. The core attractive element of citizenship in its early days—the promise of equality based on an abstract, random status assignment that infused with reason precisely random exclusion, and discrimination based on countless grounds—now haunts citizenship's attractiveness: random punishment of abstract human beings has to withstand the test of rationality and be convincing, which implies looking precisely behind the veil of the abstract, at the concrete circumstances of each case. This strikes at the very sacred heart of citizenship.

In a way, human rights protect the vulnerable noncitizens from the *intended* punitive effects of the assignment of the citizenship status. The further thinning of citizenship is thus absolutely unavoidable in this context: increasingly, many arbitrarily assigned "citizenship rights" are bound to be openly rebranded, turning into human rights or rights based on concrete factors going beyond abstract status assignment: legal residence, presence in the jurisdiction, and the like. It is fundamental to fully realize in this context that citizenship's definitional lack of dignity and its programmed-in arbitrariness make it absolutely impossible to reverse the current trend, unless the dominant contemporary ideals of human rights and fighting arbitrariness in law fade away, which is highly unlikely in the current context, despite nationalist passions and the apparent global retreat of democracy, as observed by Amichai Magen.[64] Moreover, sooner or later this trend is bound also to touch upon political rights, which trail behind at the moment and form a special case to be discussed in chapter 5.

Having reviewed the palette of citizenship rights and the crucial developments in this sphere, the main lesson one draws is that just as the importance of citizenship at the level of the status is starting to diminish, as discussed in chapter 2, at the level of rights that citizenship confers, similar processes can be observed. In the current context, citizenship inescapably fails as a persuasive tool of unquestioned exclusion. The possession of the status is no longer, indeed, following Ferrajoli, has *never* been indispensable for the enjoyment of the majority of the core rights Marshall associated with citizenship more than half a century ago. While obviously contradicting citizenship's core ideological message of equality, dignity, and justice, the developments described here in fact mean more equality and less random assignment (read deprivation) of rights. The thinning of citizenship unavoidably opens up more rights for residents as well as simply "persons" and further disturbs the acceptance of the flimsy mantras of citizenship we dismissed in chapter 2, including an assumption that citizenship comes with dignity and values; that all the citizenships in the world are essentially equal and thus incomparable; and that citizenship is justified in capping our imagination by grounding our whole existence in the context of the boundaries of the state conferring

Citizenship inescapably fails as a persuasive tool of unquestioned exclusion.

it. Importantly, the trend of decoupling citizenship and rights has prevailed worldwide.

Some jurisdictions, especially the whole of the European continent, are experiencing the continuation of the logical pressure along the same lines: as we have seen from *Beldjoudi v. France* and *Jeunesse v. Netherlands*, even the right to reside, the most sacred cow of citizenship, can be human rights-based and defy the arbitrariness lying at the core of citizenship. De facto citizenships emerge based on the private circumstances of the person concerned, with no regard to the formal legality of stay or the possession of a formal status of citizenship. Part of the same trend, questioning citizenship's definitional arbitrariness, the waning of the direct correlation between the enjoyment of such rights and the territory of the jurisdiction issuing the status, has now been broken through the rise of intercitizenships (figure 6). Citizenship rights are thus under pressure, which is truly liberating, since crucially important entitlements previously viewed as associated with citizenship are now clearly understood as rooted in grounds much more equitable and just than citizenship. Furthermore, randomness is not the core driving factor behind these grounds, thus positively distinguishing them from citizenship.

DUTIES

Besides rights and liberties, citizenship has also traditionally brought with it obligations. The very point of citizenship has traditionally been to make those in the prince's power fight his wars and pay his expenses: duties are a crucial reason behind citizenship's existence. Unlike rights, which do not necessarily need to be mentioned expressly in law, following the ancient universal legal principle of *nulla poena sine lege*—all that is not prohibited is allowed—duties do need a clear legal basis. So, as rightly suggested by Glanville Williams, while there is no entry on "breakfast, liberty to eat" in the index of the *Corpus Juris*, this does not mean that there is no such right, while jury duty needs to be clearly set out in law.[1] This permits us to enumerate the duties in question clearly, exposing a variation in approaches to the substance of the duties of citizenship in the various jurisdictions.

Different legal systems around the world diverge hugely with regard to the kinds of duties they expect their citizens to perform. The Indian constitution is one of the most detailed on this subject. Article 51A(h), for instance, requires the citizens of India "to develop the scientific temper, humanism and the spirit of inquiry and reform." By contrast, the foundational documents of the European Union fail to mention a single duty, thus bringing about none. The United States, besides jury duty, most exceptionally obliges its citizens to pay taxes no matter where they reside; Turkey and Belgium oblige their citizens to vote; the UAE and Saudi Arabia prohibit citizens from renouncing the Muslim religion;[2] Estonia, Greece, and North Korea require their citizens to join the military; and Cuba obliges citizens to stay on the island. Historically, citizen's duties varied even more—from prolific procreation in Ceaușescu's Romania, to forgetting any minority mother tongue in France and Canada, to honoring strict racial segregation in the United States a short while back. What unites pretty much all the jurisdictions in the world, from Eritrea to Panama, and however different the duties of citizenship they enforce are, is the duty to be a "good" and loyal citizen. Treason has traditionally been a punishable offense around the globe, whether you betray Her Majesty Queen Elizabeth II, "the French nation," Emperor Bocassa, the Pope and Antipope, or a Somalian pirate chief.[3] "Good citizens" do not rebel or question the status quo. Even more important, they are not indifferent and are expected to actively support the power relations of the society into which they happened to be born. The crucial moment here is that it is absolutely irrelevant how just or democratic that society seems to be to us, or, indeed, to the recipients of duties.

Upon closer inspection, the majority of citizenship duties most popular around the world besides not committing treason and joining the conscripted military (in the few countries where it still exists—see table 1) are mere proclamations with no legal enforcement or indeed substantive content: hot air. T. H. Marshall spoke of citizenship duties in a vein similar to what the Indian constitution propagates: "[Citizen's] acts should be inspired by a lively sense of responsibility towards the welfare of the community."[4] These are mere desiderata, of course, not legal obligations. That this is the case is good news, since there can be as many ideas, often mutually exclusive ones, on what "the welfare of the community" is as there are citizens. Moreover, they have nothing to do with the possession of the legal status of citizenship per se. Given that citizens' rights have a radically different nature in that those *are* enforceable in law and *do* require one to be proclaimed by the authority in charge as a citizen, there is no direct connection between the rights and duties of citizenship. This does not deprive duties of a vital function in the citizenship universe, however.

Table 1 The abolition of military conscription around the world

----

Country	Year conscription abolished
Argentina	1995
Australia	1972
Austria	still in place
Belgium	1992
Bulgaria	2008
Canada	1945
Chile	de facto voluntary service
China	de facto voluntary service
Czech Republic	2005
Egypt	still in place
France	2001
Germany	2011
India	has never been introduced
Iran	still in place
Israel	still in place
Italy	2005
Japan	1945
Kazakhstan	still in place
New Zealand	1973
North Korea	still in place
Poland	2010

Table 1 (continued)

Country	Year conscription abolished
Portugal	2004
Romania	2007
Russia	still in place
Saudi Arabia	has never been introduced
Singapore	still in place
South Korea	still in place
Spain	2001
Sweden	reintroduced in 2018
The Netherlands	1997
United Kingdom	1960
United States	1973

Duties/Rights Interactions

While the stories of a correlation between rights and duties abound, duties are rarely a part of the definition of citizenship in law—beyond the proclamation of the possible existence of duties in theory. The same is true in our common language: even the Oxford English Dictionary does not treat "citizenship" as a word with duty implications, defining it as "a position or status of being a citizen with its rights and privileges." Talk of this mythical correlation is nevertheless recurrent in writing about citizenship. This is related, as I have also argued elsewhere, to the instrumental role, which such correlation talk plays in justifying random exclusions from rights and reinforcing complacency among citizens, thus helping the status improve the governability of societies by making the public uniform and by smashing dissent, fostering obedience and complacency.[5]

What would the moral foundations of citizenship duties be? Clearly, for their respective citizens, whether you join the Israeli military or object has to do with your thoughts about the future of peace in the region and the enduring existence of the State of Israel (five years in jail if you do not); whether you vote in Belgian elections reflects your level of interest in the government and the state (an administrative fine of up to EUR 125 if you fail to show up);[6] just as whether you call Chairman Xi a "steam bun Xi" (two years in jail, if said in a private chat conversation); or protest against the annual Waffen-SS veterans march in Riga, sharing the position of the Simon Wiesenthal Centre in condemning the only such procession in Europe[7] (a warning from an administrative court with a ban on holding protests for a year)—these are all decisions reflecting personal conscience. Once citizenship duties are at play, these choices are foreclosed by law—in all these cases you are violating a duty and will be punished for thinking differently from the authorities.

Given that, as we have seen, citizenship is randomly distributed among all people and erects often impenetrable walls of inequality between and within societies, to present any duty as a necessary reflection of the bond between people living together, or an obligation of gratitude for the rights of citizenship, would probably be going a bit too far.[8] Given that the main citizenship right, as we have seen, relates to a person's lawful presence in a jurisdiction, the gratitude sought amounts to requiring that person to be grateful to whoever claims the territory for merely being allowed to live a life there. Even more important, gratitude without choice is unconvincing, especially in a world where most citizenships outside of the richest HDI-leader nations are simply a liability and rights only appear in theory. Stretching the mythical correlation even further lands us in a world where whatever legal system one is born into, however unreasonable and repugnant we might think it, deserves respect simply by virtue of being there. Possible reservations that can be found in the literature— "only if it is democratic," "only if it is just"[9]—do not resolve the core problematic point, and rather make the argument less convincing from the start. The fact that the majority of the world's citizens do not actually inhabit democratic and just—and who is to judge what "just" is?—societies is another matter.

Furthermore, presuming that unwritten duties do not exist and will not be enforceable, any legal system with no meaningful duties for citizens on its books—such as the European Union, the Netherlands, France, or the Czech Republic—would then be devoid of a basis for citizenship rights, should the correlation premise be correct. Thankfully, this is not the case and the Oxford English Dictionary is not lying—rather the ideologues of just and dignifying citizenship do. An authority may extract duties from those holding a status under its control, but the rights do not evaporate should the authority run out of inspiration and decide to rein in its appetite for such extraction.

That said, it is undeniable that citizens owe duties to the states that choose to claim such duties: given that citizenship status is totalitarian and unilateral, as we have seen, in that the person claimed has no choice in whether to submit or not, states are free to extract duties and obedience to any extent they prefer, as long as it is sustainable in terms of basic governability. Despite being exceptional in basing taxation on citizenship, the United States is still doing pretty well, notwithstanding a small but steady flow of U.S. citizenship renunciation requests from those who view such exceptionalism as unjust. In fact, only Eritrea enforces similar rules, known as a diaspora tax and a national defense fee, used according to the UN Security Council, to fund Al-Shabaab, a terrorist organization.[10] North Korea supplies another exceptional duty example: men serve ten years in its now nuclear-armed military, while women serve only until the age of 23.[11] Such onerous service might only be the beginning of the list of what the state wants from you based on the outcome of the birthright lottery. Every North Korean, like every American and every Eritrean, unsurprisingly is taught to be grateful to the state and to be proud of the country's achievements.

The flimsy foundations of any claims, especially to property, lives, and collective memory, based on any randomly assigned status are self-evident; their legitimacy stands contested. Citizenship, as a tool of governance, has been indispensable to states to create a durable perception of justice in its operation to ensure administrations function smoothly and reduce the transaction costs of the preservation of the status quo. This is why the United States remains de facto the only country that bases its taxation on citizenship alongside residence—the criterion for the rest of the world. This is also why conscription is now an exception in the world, rather than the rule.[12]

Duties of citizenship historically have played a central role in helping rationalize the irrational. However, if the economic, social, and political costs of extraction become such that they undermine the rationalizing status of duties, the duties are bound to fade away: this is precisely the trend observable the world over in recent decades. Citizenship duties are in a strong decline worldwide and the pace of the abolition of conscription is a good illustration of this one-way development.

The Violence of "Good Citizenship"

Since Bodin's critique of Aristotle, subjugation to the sovereign has been the essence of the claim to equality and a fundamental element of the status. This reasoning has not changed much since olden times, still holding true in theory from Putin's Russia to Trump's America, only now the sovereign usually is said to be "the people." Writes Bodin: "It must be said that privileges do not make a citizen. It is the acknowledgement and obedience of a free subject towards his sovereign Prince, and the guidance, justice and the defence of the Prince towards the subject which makes the citizen and which is the essential difference between a citizen and a foreigner."[13] What is interesting here, as Keechang Kim notes in his fine study, is that Bodin entirely missed the context of the Aristotelian world, where the core distinction between persons was between the free and unfree, masters and slaves—not between foreigners and citizens—and where, even more significant, there was no place for the individualist conception of citizenship. Remember, we are in the world predating St. Paul and individual salvation, which would revolutionize the idea of justice, should we believe Larry Siedentop,[14] by moving justice away from the strict apportionment of liberty, reinventing it instead as a general promise of equality among those who share faith and submit to the same ruler.

Having virtually no duties left in the context of contemporary citizenships, it is almost difficult to believe that the extraction of duties has been the leading driving factor behind the emergence of citizenship as such in the first place. The history of citizenship and its duties is best explained by Charles Tilly, who looks at the part played by coercive exploitation in the creation of European states.[15] Those who won in the wars between competing thugs achieved dominant positions as the managers of an extraction racket: one where escape was rendered almost impossible by threat of violence, allegiance was inalienable, and social conditions were such that the dangers from which protection was needed abounded through, precisely, the business of the princes constantly at war with each other. The rule of force is convincing, but the ideas of justice and administrative sophistication evolve at a rapid pace, reducing the costs of governance. Although citizenship per se is one of the most prominent inbuilt structural elements of pure arbitrariness in modern governance systems, it has rationalizations aplenty, which are never approached critically by the citizens' public. And while the unchallengeable, force-based extraction racket that citizenship used to support acquired a positive image by being clothed up with all kinds of popular ideals, the latter fail to withstand closer scrutiny. The myth of the dignity of citizenship, its intrinsic worth, and the belief that rights and duties correlate occupy a particularly important place among such tools.

Some duties are purely declaratory and serve to cement the myth of the dignity of citizenship even further. Intellectually vacant at the core, such duties actually work through the creation of a custom, involving mindless repetition, such as schoolchildren pledging allegiance to their nation's flag. Self-determination, freedom, sacrifice—all kinds of rhetoric are employed to justify the efficient governability of the domestic population, the people who are always there *without* choosing to be, in the context where an easy way out usually is not available. Moreover, even if blindly following the mantras of duties actually did happen according to one's own choosing, all it testifies to on many occasions is the moral poverty of the people concerned and their regrettable inability to form independent judgments, rather than to their good citizenship. Michael Walzer is absolutely right in regretting such misrepresentation of miserably poor judgment as a dignifying patriotic feeling: "In August 1914, Australians and Germans, Frenchmen and Englishmen, flooded the enlistment offices, but we would not want to explain their military enthusiasm by reference to the quality of their citizenship [but rather] as a sign of the poverty of their lives and their lack of moral independence."[16] In this sense it is a truism to report that those branded traitors are often more thoughtful and reasonable than the submissive mob. "America, red white and blue we spit on you," the famous chant from the flag burning protest in *Texas v. Johnson*—one of the core First

Amendment cases[17]—could thus be argued to be more patriotic than, say, enlisting to fight in Vietnam or striving to be listed among the heroes of the Iraq war, as much as one can be in any way a hero these days in the context of the atrocities based on falsehoods, exemplified best by the 2003 General Powell's speech at the UN Security Council that misinformed the world about Iraq's weapons of mass destruction, which led to unprecedented devastation for no clear and legally acceptable reason.[18] The story of unpatriotic traitors failing to perform their duty is the same all over, from the Christmas bonding across the trenches on the Western front in 1914 to Rosa Parks claiming her seat on a bus in 1955, or the countless whistleblowers, from Mordechai Vanunu, who spent two decades in solitary confinement in Israeli jails for going public about the country's nuclear program, to Edward Snowden and Chelsea Manning exposing U.S. government surveillance of its citizens and military and diplomatic documents. Any violation of a "duty," especially if it implies treason, exposes the citizen to overwhelming pressure and state violence. It could, however, also constitute an act of heroism. Punishing traitors almost always translates into smashing dissent and trivializing it—whatever the reasons underpinning it—with an appeal to the irrational: national dignity, glory, destiny. These are protected with reference to national security. The sliding of Turkey into totalitarianism over recent years, with thousands arrested on accusations of

Punishing traitors
almost always translates
into smashing dissent
and trivializing it.

being involved in a coup against the grandly dictatorial Erdoğan, is a clear example of this, just as McCarthyism was with its anti-communist craze.[19] Citizens are constantly punished the world over in democracies, autocracies, and theocracies alike, into believing that there is no truth behind Jefferson's (most likely apocryphal) wisdom that "dissent is patriotic."

Not everyone is a hero, of course. The best way to avoid the choice between individual judgment and extreme violence is to get rid of the citizenship status, should the option be available. Albert Einstein's citizenship story is an excellent illustration of a masterful use of this option: the great American left his native Kingdom of Württemberg in 1896 to rid himself of its nationality to make sure no draft call disrupted his life and his studies, moved to Switzerland, and naturalized there, to proceed to do the same in the United States in 1940, fleeing Nazi Germany.[20] The legendary singer-songwriter Carlos Gardel offers another example: if you ask an Argentinian friend why she thinks the great Gardel lied about his place of birth and registered in 1920 as a Uruguayan, the ensuing heated conversation could go on all night. The likely answer, as a biographer claims, was to avoid the military obligations of Gardel's French and Argentinian citizenships.[21] Those like Gardel, Einstein, and countless others who brave the glorified complacency narrative are usually despised by the state and, unquestionably, by the "good citizens" who inhabit and reinforce the official narrative. Many states make it difficult to renounce citizenship before fulfilling military service or other duties, where these are present. Any American who is thought to have renounced citizenship to avoid paying taxes becomes "inadmissible" to the country.[22]

It is true, however, that exit is usually not an option or made extremely difficult. Citizens have to obey, blending in, or suffer: they must turn out for elections in Belgium even if they have no interest in Belgian politics; man blockposts in the settlements in Gaza, even if they consider the Israeli occupation illegal; refrain from protesting against SS veteran marches in the middle of Latvia's capital, even if they believe the SS to be a despicable criminal organization. Holding the photograph of SS troops killing Jews in Latvia next to the street where the honored SS veterans were due to march in 2017 was condemned by a Latvian court in the case of *Šaripovs* as a clear departure from good citizenship ideals:

> It follows from the factual circumstances described in the protocol, that A. Šaripovs had used a placard depicting violence, thus propagating violence …
>
> On the placard used by A. Šaripovs during the picket, the violence of a kind that a military organization is using, violence against prisoners of war, is depicted. Taking into account that the picket

was organized by A. Šaripovs exactly on March the 16th, a part of the society undeniably connects those soldiers with Waffen SS military organization, where ethnic Latvians had served, among others ...

Public display of such inimical and violent photo images, which promote national hatred in the society, can undeniably cause mass riots, which can lead to further destabilisation of the political situation and a transfer of the socio-political and economic tensions present in the society to interethnic relations ...

Public display of such photo images is closely connected with discrediting the image of Latvia internationally. Taking into account the high tension in the public, international resonance, historical situation and blatant violence depicted on the placards, in order to defend public order and safety, democratic state order, and to avoid deliberate confrontation, it is found that A. Šaripovs needs to be punished.[23]

One of the two core functions of the duties of citizenship traditionally has been the uniformization of the citizenry, the reproduction of complacency, and the necessary uprooting of individuality and dissent: a reality that marks democracies and totalitarian regimes alike. This is because any authority in the world has traditionally tasked itself— and to a large extent still tasks itself—with the creation of a "good citizen." Only a "good," not a "bad" citizen is worthy of the motherland's attention and love. Never mind if such love is unwanted. Even more, those citizens who are not "good" usually would either be proclaimed not to exist, just like lesbians in the eyes of Queen Victoria, or actively be suppressed by the powers that be, dismissed as lazy, ignorant, and criminal.

The core duty of citizenship then—the one necessarily found in all the legal systems around the world—has always been to be a good citizen: to blend into the state-sponsored narrative. This duty is part of what citizenship is, going to the core of the status and supporting its main function. Who is a good citizen? Here totalitarian regimes and democracies—indeed, any authority custodian of a citizenship status—converge: the good citizen is one who upholds and reinforces the predominant status quo in society and fits neatly into the stereotypes of a worthy life lived with dignity as spelled out in prevailing social conventions and enforced by law. The disruptors, otherwise called bad citizens, are punished.

Most important, and building further on the necessarily totalitarian essence of the status of citizenship—just as with the distribution of the status as such—it will be up to the relevant authority to decide exactly what is good and what is bad. Advocating free love, helping fugitive slaves (or refugees, for that matter, which is a punishable offense in contemporary Hungary, among other countries), or attempting to vote as a woman can be as bad in the eyes of the authorities as writing Nobel Prize-winning poetry. The most theatrical illustration of this played out at a session of the Dzerzhinsky District Court—strangely, actually sitting on stage for the occasion—in the City of Leningrad on February 18, 1964, at a trial for the "social parasitism" of citizen Joseph Brodsky, who failed to make his due contribution to society (transcribed by Frida Vigdorova):[24]

Judge: What do you do for living?

Brodsky: I write poetry. I translate. I suppose ...

Judge: Never mind what you "suppose." Stand up properly. Don't lean against the wall. Look at the court. Answer the court properly. Do you have a regular job?

Brodsky: I thought this was a regular job.

Judge: Answer correctly!

Brodsky: I was writing poems. I thought they'd be published. I suppose ...

Judge: We are not interested in "suppose." Tell us why you weren't working. ... And in general, what is your specific occupation?

Brodsky: Poet. Poet-translator.

Judge: And who said you are a poet? Who ranked you among poets?

Brodsky: No one. Who ranked me as a member of the human race?

Judge: Did you study for this?

Brodsky: Study for what?

Judge: To become a poet. Did you attend some university where people are trained … where they're taught …

Brodsky: I didn't think it was a matter of education.

Judge: How, then?

Brodsky: I think that … (*perplexed*) it comes from God …

Judge: Do you have any petitions to the court?

Brodsky: I'd like to know why I was arrested.

Judge: That's a question, not a petition. … Citizen Brodsky … explain to the court why you didn't work … and why you led a parasitical way of life.

Brodsky: I did just what I am doing now: I wrote poems.

Judge: That is, you wrote your so-called poems? What was the purpose of your changing your place of work so often? … How were you useful to the motherland?

Brodsky: I wrote poems. That's my work. I'm convinced ... I believe that what I've written will be of use to people not only now, but also to future generations.

Judge: That is you think that your so-called poems are of use to people?

Brodsky: Why do you say my poems are "so-called" poems?

Judge: We refer to your poems as "so-called" because we have no other impression of them ...

Public Prosecutor Sorokin: Brodsky is defended by rogues, parasites, lice, and beetles. He's not a poet, but just a man trying to write verse. He's forgotten that in our society man must work, must create something of value: machine tools, bread, or poems. Brodsky must be compelled to work. He must be sent away from this Hero City. He's a parasite, a lout, a rogue, and an ideologically filthy man. His admirers merely spatter their saliva. But Nekrasov said: "You may choose not to be a poet /But you cannot choose not to be a citizen" ...

Judge: Brodsky has systematically failed to fulfill the obligations of a Soviet citizen with regard to producing material value and personal well-being, which is apparent from his changing jobs frequently. ... From the report of the commission of work with young writers it is clear that Brodsky is not a poet. Readers of the newspaper *Evening Leningrad* have condemned him. Therefore the court has decided to apply the decree dated 4 February 1961: Brodsky will be sent to remote locations for a period of five years of forced labour.

It is crucial to understand that the duties of citizenship, although significantly diverging in scale, work in exactly the same way in democratic and totalitarian societies: their functions are too important and too ancient to be disturbed by the nature of the political regime in power. On this count, being guilty of writing verse is identical in essence to holding a photograph depicting SS atrocities at a patriotic celebration of Nazi troops in Riga, to being unwilling to kill Afghans and Vietnamese half the globe away, to keeping secrets about potentially criminal behavior of your own state, or to deciding not to show up at elections in Belgium. Through the proclaimed duties, which are always harshly policed, citizenship emerges as the force opposing societal innovation, inclusion, and dignity.

As societies change, the mainstream idea of the acceptable changes equally. What remains stable through all such changes is that "good citizenship" is there to stay and with its duties and the punishments associated with failing to perform them, it is rarely, if ever, socially progressive. Crucially, those people who are branded as "bad citizens" are not only outright criminals or those who propose novel ideals and push for the widening of the idea of equality, inclusion, and rights, but also those who are indifferent to the official ideology, be it a particular form of democracy, theocracy, or communist totalitarianism. The indifferent have to be educated (or reeducated) to turn out to vote for the European Parliament,[25] to love the Communist Party, to put a swastika ornament on the Christmas tree, to not skip church—and so on. A good citizen is thus *actively complacent*: an Eagle Scout, a Hitler Jügend leader, a public morality vigilante in Iran. He joins voluntary associations, which is something the British citizenship law, without a hint of any irony, expects of those willing to naturalize.[26] He changes his beliefs when necessary, switching almost overnight, like the Romanian elites, from loudly advocating Ceaușescu's communist dogmas to kissing the hands of Orthodox Church leaders.[27] Someone, like Brodsky, who genuinely did not care about the allegations of being a "parasite," later confessing that he was deeply preoccupied by a strain in the relationship with his lover and barely followed the absurd trial, thus becomes as bad a citizen as Dr. Martin Luther King Jr., who confronted the powers that be. A display of indifference, in the eyes of these powers, often equals rebellion. Thinking of love at a show trial clearly made Brodsky unworthy of Soviet citizenship, which he was stripped of upon going into exile. Similarly, Andrei Tarkovsky, in the *Martyrologue*, his diaries, struggled with the negative reaction of the Soviet authorities to his decision to stay in Italy to work, not for political reasons. What he did not see is that active complacency is always indispensable: it is the synonym of good citizenship, the explanation, in some legal systems such as those of Turkey or Belgium, for punishing those who do not care about politics and refuse to show up at elections they possibly do not believe in. The 1981 British Nationality Act (in force until 2002) used to give active complacency absolute prominence, allowing for the annulment of the citizenship of any subject "disloyal or *disaffected* to his Majesty."[28] Such affection is nurtured the world over, from national anthems at sporting events to national flags in churches.

The picture changes, of course, after the rebels win: they suddenly become great citizens, even heroes. General George Washington, Vladimir Lenin, or South Sudan's Salva Kiir Mayardit with his ten-gallon hat are suddenly leaders in the spotlight. Those who did not care, always a majority, never emerge victorious, and are thus constantly despised, lumped together with those who failed. The main enemy of good citizenship is thus the right to be left alone, to exist outside of actively professed ideology, which totalitarian societies, just like liberal democracies, see as a serious problem to tackle, a sign of the lack of maturity, poor education, or a failure to understand. The EU institutions, constantly puzzled by citizens' disinterest in

European Parliament elections, are a great example of this, bemoaning Europeans' lack of knowledge: the indifferent are presented as simpletons. This view is understandable, since the indifferent are the most dangerous threat to any claims of the legitimacy of power. No leader—either democratic or a totalitarian—can fully rely on those who do not care even if dissent is suppressed.

Active complacency is promoted through the forging of exclusionary togetherness: brotherhood in a conscript army, national history competitions at school, museums telling national stories: "ancient Belorussians lived on these swamps since 7,000 years"; "this Byzantine church is built in the Macedonian style since the Empire was then run by ancient Macedonians"; civil religion and state rituals, from a pledge of allegiance every morning at school, to a grumpy remark addressed to someone not Italian enough to order a cappuccino after lunch in Florence. "Good" is broad and touches the nerves at the very core of every imagined community. Its policing is as state-mandated as it is socially ingrained, dependent on well-meaning vigilantes.

The well-meaning citizens who do the right thing are glorified. Research suggests that *all* the cases against "Aryan" Germans cohabiting with "Jewish" women were started based on information from coworkers, neighbors, and family members.[29] A good citizen of the Reich was educated through the media and legal discourse to avoid

Rassenschande—race defilement—and care about "honor," which later morphed into the key principle of dignity in contemporary German and EU law, as James Whitman has demonstrated.[30] Once again: the skeptics, the rebels, and the indifferent will be on the receiving side of violence and indignation, failing to fulfill the core duty of complacency: being actively "good" on the terms the authorities define. Reeducation is always an option, as Nazi race-defilement laws demonstrate—or U.S. punishments for miscegenation enforced long after World War II ended. Szobar reports Third Reich court cases where the "uneducated Aryan" defendants received the court's pity for not being able to make the fine racial distinctions required by the law: "the witness ... has blue eyes and blond hair. These features obscure her Jewish racial characteristics so strongly that a lay person will have difficulty recognizing her as Jewish."[31] The state demands good citizens, whom it creates, to see and enforce legal distinctions it introduces, which is the vital part of what Pierre Bourdieu called the "practical activity of 'world-making' (marriages, divorces, substitutions, associations, dissolutions) which constitutes social units. Law is the quintessential form of the symbolic power of naming that creates the things named, and creates social groups in particular,"[32] including "Aryan" citizens, "Jewish" Germans, and "Latino" Americans. Being racist in all aspects of life, including its most private corners, was thus the core feature of a good German citizen.

"World-making" goes much deeper than simply outlining the legal and illegal—it drives the majority conceptions of right and wrong affecting our identity and often outlasts a prohibition itself: anti-Semitism is still strong in many European countries, even though it has long since ceased to be required by law; PornHub research still speaks of the popularity of "interracial sex" porn in the southern states of the United States, even though miscegenation is no longer a legal taboo.[33]

Justification of Discrimination

Besides forging a "good citizen," who is meek and obedient, and is ready to die for the authorities when requested, there is a second interconnected function with which the duties of citizenship are entrusted. Such duties have traditionally been justifying discrimination and the failure to extend the rights of citizenship to all. Since the authority in charge of citizenship, as we have seen, has an overwhelming power to decide who is a citizen among the bodies available, as well as the meaning of "good" and "bad" citizenship, it has absolute discretion to determine in law the *citizens' abilities*. This point is crucial: fulfilling the duty of being good does not so much mean that you do all that is expected of you as an actively complacent and status quo-loving citizen. You should also be granted the theoretical ability in law to do precisely that by the official thinking about your legally defined kind as a member of a group. As we have seen, a woman's giving birth to a child does not necessarily produce a citizen—by law, she could not pass on the status in most of the world's jurisdictions until very recently. An African American joining a U.S. militia in the nineteenth century is not necessarily capable of defending his country—by law, he was not good enough to join the ranks, since only "white able-bodied men" were proclaimed worthy enough to join.[34] A Japanese American in the 1940s could not be loyal—again, by law—no matter what he actually thinks and believes in.[35] A contemporary Muslim citizen everywhere in the Western world is a potential terrorist, as Christian Joppke has shown.[36] Using the rights-duties correlation in a context where citizens' features and abilities are determined either explicitly or implicitly by law, incorporating, installing, and reenacting public prejudice is a powerful rhetorical device in this universe of legal truths to justify the non-extension of rights. Chief Justice Taney in *Dred Scott*—probably the most infamous decision in the history of the U.S. Supreme Court—provided the reasoning that explains this function of the duties of citizenship best. Since service in the militia is limited by law to a "free able-bodied white male citizen," "the African race" is "repudiated, and rejected from the duties and obligations of citizenship."[37] On this account where there are no duties, there are no rights.

The whole story behind the fight for nondiscrimination and the inclusion of women, minorities, and resident non-citizens into the ambit of the traditional rights of citizenship has progressed in crucial ways along the lines of the possible, as it is legally marked out by the powers that be. So women were said to be "too weak" to be helpful in the military. In recognition of this weakness first proclaimed and then enforced in law, they were exempt from the citizenship duty of defending the country. And in a world where the duties and rights of citizenship were said to correlate, it was only logical that women should not vote or benefit from other citizenship rights. Duties thus emerged as a potent justification for discriminating among citizens.

The logic of discrimination was so ingrained that the way to gain access to rights lay through the legally constrained world of the proclaimed possible. American women would argue that they should be allowed the vote because they produce soldiers and suffer from grief once those soldiers die in fulfilment of their duties of citizenship.[38] This suffering elevated women to a level qualifying them to benefit from the rights their citizenship status has to offer, thus remedying their legally proclaimed uselessness as the dischargers of citizenship duties in law. The struggle to get to this point lasted at least seventy years in the United States—from the 1848 call for a Woman's Rights Convention until the ratification of the Nineteenth

Duties thus emerged as
a potent justification
for discriminating
among citizens.

Amendment in 1920. The duties of citizenship are fundamental to justifying the reproduction of irrational discriminations through the strict application of citizenship, an official status of equals.

The reinforcement and embedding of complacency and the justification of humiliation and exclusion from rights are the two main functions of citizenship duties since their debut. As we have seen, three factors led to the articulation of this pair of functions: the authority in charge monopolized not only the distribution of the status of citizenship—in other words, who in the society will exist in full in the eyes of the law—but also of its identitarian aspect, the idea of a good citizen. The latter came with the determination by law of the limits of the skills and abilities of different groups of citizens in a society. The belief in the correlation between the rights and duties of citizenship provided a crucial connection between the authority's monopoly to deny minority groups the ability to contribute, while simultaneously justifying discrimination against them. Both the reproduction of complacency and the solid justification of discrimination were essentially important tools deployed by citizenship as a tool of governability.

The significance of the two functions of citizenship duties dramatically diminished, however, in the late twentieth century. They simply ceased to be generally acceptable in the context of the opening up of the status of citizenship, the cumulation of such statuses, and the rise in the popularity of the human rights ideology, which questioned the authorities' determinations. Purely legal truths gave way to looking at the actual situation on the ground, exposing the duties' flaws in the world of contemporary citizenship. As the preservation of discrimination within any given legal system ceased to be the core function of citizenship, the duties of citizenship, which enabled this function, started disappearing.

The Duties' Revolutions

Revisiting these developments it is possible to say that citizenship duties in the twentieth century went through three revolutions. The first is a definitive choice for taxation based on residence as opposed to allegiance. By taxing residents as opposed to citizens, all the countries in the world except for the United States and Eritrea diminished their transaction costs in extracting revenues and acquired a powerful justification for taxation, rationalizing it through presence in the state—which is presented as a matter of choice—as opposed to citizenship, which is a random ascription. Paying taxes, outside of the United States, is not a citizenship duty because it is residence based.

The second duties' revolution flows from what Michael Howard potently characterized as "the invention of peace," which is much more innovative than it may sound.[39] As Charles Tilly has convincingly argued, "Over the long run, far more than other activities, war and preparation for war produced the major components of European states"[40]—it is thus not by chance that conscription and the duty of joining the military played such an inflated role in the construction of citizenship and subjugation of the populations: nationalism emerged as one of the most effective ways to motivate the masses to die without asking about the cause. Once peace, not war, became the starting point for international relations, following the condemnation of war with the founding of the United Nations, military technology and the public perception of service evolved, making conscript armies unnecessary. War-making, among the most developed states at least, is now a profession, as dignifying as any other. Building a career as a good citizen through seeking glory on a battlefield is all but impossible, not merely somewhat old-fashioned. In the age of peace marked by post-heroic geopolitics, wars are no longer fought between the "peoples."[41] Civilians, as Howard underlined, rather than being an enthusiastic reservoir of manpower, have turned into simple hostages. The changing role of civilians, or the majority of the citizenry throughout this shift marked by the invention of peace is remarkable: when nations are at war as opposed to states, the law treated every "enemy alien" as potentially dangerous: the first half of the twentieth century from World War I onward was the apogee of this kind of thinking: "enemy origins" led to mass denaturalizations, while resident foreigners from the countries on the other side of the trenches had to leave their homes and were treated as enemies—including of course all the local women, who lost their citizenship upon marrying enemy foreigners, and whom Daniela Cagliotti described in her research.[42]

Modern professional soldiers of the Western world are the killers of men and women,[43] usually in much less prosperous societies, upholding and reinforcing the dramatic divide between the former colonizing powers and the former colonials. Former colonial subjects are actively used in such wars in fact, often lured by a prospect of a citizenship status greatly superior to their own. The Spanish legion is composed of non-citizens, just like the French *Legion Etrangère*, (Foreign Legion), which is composed of foreigners without an identity. The U.S. military has been eagerly embracing foreigners too. Compare this to the societies where citizenship duties in their classical sense remained "more meaningful": the South African army was 100 percent white South Africans during the time of apartheid[44] and the conscript army of the Estonian republic is composed 100 percent of citizens in a divided society where a significant share of the population is deemed ethnically unfit for citizenship and thus also for service or equal rights.

The post-heroic age did not begin yesterday, of course, and had its well-known heroes. Sir Basil Zaharoff, to give one example, was knighted for services to the war industry in the UK, but the patent he held for the Maxim machine gun brought dividends from any slaughter anywhere on the globe, helping all parties win as much as it helped all parties lose. Sir Basil, glorified and honored by the winners of the war, was of course not your common good citizen. In fact, he probably did not care at all who would win, like the poet Brodsky, but his inspiration was profit, not poetry.[45] He emerges, however, as a much more thoughtful and able individual than those pitied by Michael Walzer, who queued at enlistment points to die on all sides out of nationalist hate under fire from Sir Basel's profitable guns. Complacency, the main virtue citizenship has traditionally tried to promote, enabled countless disasters. It also made sure that the predator states of the twentieth century functioned smoothly. Indeed, to turn to Walzer again, the decline in the duties of citizenship one observes in every single developed country today is "not a decline in civil virtue, but the working of liberal values."[46]

The third, interrelated, and most important duties revolution is the rise precisely of a tolerant attitude among states toward their own citizens with the ascent of the culture of liberalism. Although many countries still do it, it is no longer indispensable per se to break citizens and purge them of their individuality in order for them to qualify as "good" and "worthy." As Christian Joppke explains, echoing Walzer, "In a liberal society, the ties that bind can only be thin and procedural, not thick and substantive. Otherwise individuals could not be free."[47] In part this is due to the fact that France has already turned "peasants into Frenchmen" and the forging of the Chinese and the Italians duly followed their respective states' creations.[48] In addition to a reduction in the need, the decrease in the focus of "making the people" can also be explained through the rise in human rights and the ideals of minority protection. In fact, although constantly promoted of course, the complacency pillar of citizenship is no longer blindly embraced as an unquestionable value, and is sometimes dressed in other garb. The world is witnessing a rise in the protection of minorities of all kinds, with the emergence in the words of Will Kymlicka of "multicultural citizenship."[49] All kinds of identities, from gays to Rastafarians, the speakers of Friesian, vegans, and Satanists, have come to be officially recognized by the authorities in the liberal democracies. Such recognition often signifies endowment with real enforceable rights, as opposed to merely enjoying the abstractions of equality inhabiting the traditional world of citizenship. In short: the modern world is much less a world of citizen standardization and abstraction than it used to be. Human rights ideology, the belief in the value of peace, and the acknowledgment of the real individual as opposed to mass-produced and elusive "good citizen" identities, have made the duties of citizenship irrelevant: they are left to be tools in a toolbox for the perfection of the machinery of humiliation, complacency, and reasoned exclusion, where the reasoning of course is flawed.

While all this seems to be good news for all, the developments described are profoundly disruptive for the classical understanding of citizenship, while at the same time not necessarily reducing its potential for rationalizing state violence. Equality rooted in abstractness being citizenship's core starting point, individualizing the access to rights through the recognition of minority identities makes complacency and exclusion much more difficult to justify. Even more, the development in the world of citizenship that essentially led in most of contemporary democracies to the erasure of duties—now unnecessary—from the vital catalogue of citizenship's elements, unquestionably signals the diminishing relevance of the concept of citizenship as such—sexist, racist, and complacent—in the world today. No state will ever admit this openly, since states rely on the concept, but the disappearance of duties from the books is a sufficient reminder of what is actually going on: citizenship, for the first time in centuries, is becoming less totalitarian and oppressive and more inclusive, thus losing its crucial features and functions. It is essential that duties cannot easily return, unless liberal values and the human rights ideology serving them are to be suppressed. This is not to say that the idea of complacency behind good citizenship has receded: political correctness and the enforcement of the universal respect for the multiple individualisms seems to supply its substance, policed by the state: contemporary citizenship comes with a duty of embracing a very particular vision of tolerance.

Given that the dangers for classical citizenship are clear, states are trying to fight back but cannot do so effectively, since the whole context has changed. The one instance where the moves to reinstate the duties narrative are particularly pronounced is the regulation of naturalization. New citizens are subjected to tests and narratives of national exceptionalism. Too bad these all come down to the *one* and *only* value capable of being tested in modern democracies: tolerance. Anything else would go against the liberal values underpinning contemporary liberal regimes. In fact, following a conflict, precisely, with the liberal value of tolerance, a citizenship test designed by one of the Federal German Lands that tested the feelings and the actual worldviews of aspirant Germans-to-be had to be completely redesigned.[50] Tolerance being the main liberal ideal, such tests are expectedly impermissible: the testing of sacred tolerance cannot of itself be intolerant, ideally at least, turning into a farce. Citizenship tests focused on tolerance thus test the archenemy of the classical understanding of citizenship as an official status for all forced on the population by the state, which no one is in the position to refuse.

POLITICS

The political component of citizenship, alongside the principle of equality, traditionally is presented as essential to understanding what citizenship is and why it is necessary. Indeed, politics and equality are intimately connected, as the Greek word *politiká*—rooted in *politēs*, meaning "citizen"—itself suggests. The equality citizenship promises mostly crystallizes in the status holders having equal access to the ballot box, not necessarily in other aspects of life. This is particularly true given the detachment of the most civil and social rights from citizenship status. As we have seen, determining who is a citizen as well as who will be the recipient of rights and who will be subjected to duties are contested political decisions, which never simply overlap with the population of a state, however alluring the facile idea of territoriality and a territory's neatly defined settled population might seem. Consequently, just as by their definition citizens and residents never fully overlap, the same disconnect also applies to the potential overlap of citizens and voters, as well as voters and residents, as illustrated in figure 7 using the examples of Japan, Ireland, Latvia, New Zealand, St. Kitts and Nevis, the United Arab Emirates, and the United States. This unquestionably undermines the territoriality paradigm behind state-sponsored self-determination through citizenship claims. As opposed to tribal borders—which trace rituals, linguistic inflections, the shape of one's eyes and beliefs about history—territorial borders follow rivers, mountains, and geographical maps. The resulting picture is relatively complex, providing an important reality check for the usual story of the political rights of citizenship: as we shall see, the grand narrative of equal political participation could also be shorthand for tribalism and oppression.

The political side of citizenship is probably its darkest, splitting many societies, such as those of Latvia and the UAE, depicted in figure 7, down the middle. Most crucially, it elevates arbitrary exclusion to a widely accepted norm through appeals to a palette of liberty, equality, and freedom. Citizens are free, the story goes, since they belong to the political community that ensures their self-government. It is the preservation of the political community, with its presumably vibrant democratic life and the upholding of the clear set of values it espouses, that is most routinely offered as the key justification for closure, perpetuating

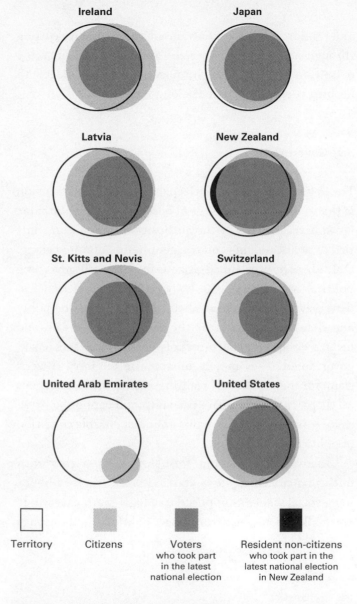

Ireland   **Japan**

Latvia   **New Zealand**

St. Kitts and Nevis   **Switzerland**

United Arab Emirates   **United States**

Territory   Citizens   Voters
who took part
in the latest
national election   Resident non-citizens
who took part in the
latest national election
in New Zealand

Figure 7   Citizenship, political rights, and territory

and reinforcing the citizen/non-citizen boundary cutting through every society. Closure—returning to Brubaker's definition—is of course the raison d'être of citizenship, keeping those who "do not belong" at bay.

Self-Government

The key presumption of citizenship's political dimension is that only citizens—those in possession of the totalitarian status conferred by the authority in charge—are entitled to political rights and can genuinely claim "to belong." Only officially proclaimed citizens form the self-governing political community—the body politic. Non-citizen residents, even if they spent their entire lives in the polity and share with its citizens the same streets, meals, and beds, are the sorry spectators of such glorious acts of self-government. They merely inhabit the territory citizens claim for themselves, officially having no say in what goes on there. Non-citizens are thus not (and cannot be) "free" as long as citizenship remains an indispensable condition of political participation.

Instead of extending formal political rights without using citizenship as a starting point, thereby honoring a social reality as opposed to a legal truth that would erase all non-citizens from view, political rights usually are reserved solely for the bearers of citizenship status. I emphasize *formal* political rights because however counterintuitive this may seem, democracy thrives far away from the ballot boxes, as Mueller and numerous others have explained:[1] non-citizens (and even non-residents in fact) can write op-eds, hire lobbyists, and give money to political causes and candidates. The list of elections and political campaigns won by foreign—"non-citizen" in our context—money and influence is very long, and gets longer every year.[2] The separation between influencing the democratic outcomes through voting and otherwise therefore is very thin indeed. As worrisome as it is, if not de jure then de facto democratic governance *is* in fact directly dependent on many factors beyond the standard narratives one finds in introductory political science texts. Charisma and money can easily outdo reason and common good.[3] Once this basic reality is considered, fetishization of regular elections as the key way to citizens' "freedom" and "self-determination" should be strongly qualified.

Exceptions to admitting solely citizen-status holders to the ballot—such as allowing New Zealand resident non-citizens or Commonwealth citizens settled in the UK to participate in national elections, or allowing EU citizens outside their home state to participate in municipal elections—are relatively rare.[4] Political participation thus offers a strong counter-narrative to the trends in

The list of elections and political campaigns won by foreign—"non-citizen" in our context—money and influence is very long, and gets longer every year.

citizenship rights outlined in chapter 3, because the decoupling of rights and citizenship has not happened in this domain of politics. Indeed, the importance of the possession of citizenship status is omnipresent here, contrary to what we have observed in the context of civil and social rights.

There is a twist to this story, however. What is significant—and counterintuitive—is that the beneficiaries of political rights increasingly include those citizens who have chosen to *leave* the territorial community where self-governance takes place and to reside elsewhere, retaining the political rights and thus taking part in governing those left behind "at home" while not being subjected to the same laws. This points to a development worth pondering: the body politic—a legal fiction established to legitimize governance of a territory—is gradually being decoupled precisely from territoriality. It thus defies its own justification and its essential reason for existing. Non-citizens are excluded from the political community in the name of citizens' self-determination. But, as we shall see, in a world where governance is overwhelmingly territorial, such self-determination cannot be secured through those leaving a community retaining their political rights, which points only to the growing irrelevance of the self-determination argument in a context where the body politic is no longer territorial, while governance is.

This picture becomes more problematic still, once the insights of chapter 2, on status, are taken on board: the body politic is not about values, since citizenship is a random totalitarian ascription, immune to choice, rendering empty all arguments grounded in the "values" citizenship is said to defend.

At the same time, values and self-governance aside, the sanctification of the connection between citizenship and political rights is not surprising. Without clinging to the ideological divide, however unconvincingly framed, between the actual lived community and the body politic of citizens as proclaimed by an authority, justifying citizenship in the contemporary context would be exceedingly problematic, if not outright impossible. Consequently, we constantly encounter the story of the crucial importance of the boundary of citizenry in the context of the political community—as opposed to the immigration boundary—shaping the actual society people make up, governed by citizens. People have sound reasons for clinging to this popular notion. Historically, the equal political rights citizens enjoyed played a critical role in winning support for the status. Indeed, the ideal of the political equality of citizens played an important liberating role in the past, when the promise of legal equality was a direct affront to the rigid caste structures enforced by law. Yet this line of argument has always been fictitious: political rights have traditionally been de facto and de jure, a forbidden terrain for women and minorities, and would barely exist in the colonies. Any justification for exclusion based on self-determination thus was never applicable to those excluded in the world and always subjected to the whims of a small clique of abstractly "free" who were far away— white male citizens behind the political machinery of the colonialism.

The Western world of the past where the official story of equality played a crucial liberating role is best illustrated, following James Q. Whitman, by the dueling codes of the day:[5] a baron had no need to kill a servant in a duel, since whatever a servant said or did couldn't amount to an offence, so inferior was the servant's position, so nonexistent his dignity. A woman, to give a more radical example, was exclusively an object, never a subject of such an honorable world. Nevertheless, the promise of equality, going hand in hand with the discovery of "honor" for all those belonging to the "people," was thus an important progressive factor, a true mobilizer in the building of contemporary societies. Looking beyond the official nationalist narrative, however, reveals a much more nuanced picture, where this enthusiasm for equality was deployed to humiliate the women and the weak, and those "not from here," in the name of the value of the democratic self-determination of the chosen few.

The citizens' self-determination narrative is problematic.[6] First, this narrative interprets away the involuntary, totalitarian nature of association underpinning citizenship. Second, it takes arbitrary status-based exclusion—both between societies and within a given society—for granted, upholding and reinforcing it, just as T. H. Marshall did, rather than problematizing it. The story of citizenship is usually presented very simply: whatever citizenship you are ascribed by law—for example, Norwegian or Pakistani—is valuable, since it allows for the articulation of collective self-determination in a political community. This freedom is achieved at least partly through the exclusion of others, even those living next door and born in the same country. Whether your citizenship is a bundle of rights or a nasty liability is irrelevant on this count, as is whether you live "at home" or "abroad": you should be happy with what you have, while allowing others to discriminate against you in the societies where you are proclaimed by law not to belong. The standard citizenship narrative, with respect to all its glories, turns into an ode to meekness and submission based on a narrative, which cannot make any sense per se across the citizenship status border.

Importantly, it makes no difference whether you are a foreigner in Qatar, South Africa, or the United States, whether you are in a minority or a majority, or, indeed, whether democracy exists in the country at all. Whoever rules the country and however the country is ruled, the defense of "common values" is always an excellent argument. Foreignness is always ascribed by law and always hurts, preempting any arguments of belonging outside the scope of exceptional *Beldjoudi v. France* and *Jeunesse v. Netherlands* situations carved out from the monolith of global assumptions by the European Court of Human Rights, as we saw when we discussed citizenship rights. Beyond such exceptions, the picture is crystal clear: as an excluded intruder you should respect others' self-determination, no matter whether democracies exist in place and however much the locals are actually oppressed by their totalitarian rulers. It does not matter of course whether you were excluded yesterday, since birth, or from the moment of entering a particular country "legally" or "illegally." Only the citizenship boundary matters for politics. The body politic is official shorthand for a yes/no question, where the answer rests on arbitrary distribution, as we have seen, rather than values and personal will.

The self-determination narrative is very robust. It successfully sustains countless counterintuitive claims, usually singling out minorities as being "not from here" and thus not entitled to the freedom of self-determination shared by all the "real" citizens. The same obviously applies to newcomers, who usually have to naturalize to partake in the self-determination exercise. It is obvious that such naturalization, if at all possible, will not be easy and could take years to achieve, in full knowledge that all the other members of the same political community around the newcomer received the status with no effort through ascription at birth. The same story repeats itself infinitely at different times on different continents. Naturalization is presented as necessary to "defend" the political community and sometimes is expected of the minorities born in a country. The reasoning that some Cambodian citizens are "not the rightful holders of the status," since their ancestors are not from Cambodia but from "somewhere else," led to the annulment of the citizenships of 100,000 members of ethnic minorities in the country in the fall of 2017. Everyone, whose passport is annulled by her own state is immediately rendered stateless and illegal. In the words of a high official: "they need to pay for illegally living here."[7] In fact, the "from somewhere else" argument always points to a minority group and is accepted as sufficient to dehumanize and exclude.

Richer countries are more sophisticated in their deployment of the "from somewhere else" argument. The officials of the newly created Czech Republic implied, for instance, that the Roma minorities should not receive Czech citizenship upon the division of the united Czechoslovakia since they were only there as a result of a successful implementation of the Czechoslovak national "Roma dispersal scheme." The scheme aimed at dispersing equally throughout the country the Roma who survived the Nazi Holocaust only in the Slovak lands, as Marc Brown reported: the Roma Holocaust in the Protectorate of Bohemia and Moravia, as the Czech Republic was called under the German occupation, was particularly brutal, meaning that the Roma "dispersed" after the war were no doubt "Slovaks."[8] The political self-determination of the Czech nation upon the division of Czechoslovakia thus implied the need to deport all the Roma to the newly formed Slovakia as "foreigners." This story tells us all we need to know about the value of the self-determination argument—it always appeals to and is addressed to those who are "in"; the others would of course not have a say. Whether the Roma in the Czech Republic agreed to be Slovaks instead of Czechs upon the split is irrelevant: the political self-articulation of the Czech nation is not dependent on the minorities' thinking and preferences. The same of course applies to all the other nations in the world: even the most tolerant constitutionalism is based on exclusion and taking sides.[9]

The glories of self-determination are not as convincing anymore, indeed, they tend to appear in a somewhat cynical light, once the story of the status is thought through seriously. Crucially, any self-determination narrative is built on a claim by a community based on birth and territory—from ancient Athenians with their myth of autochthonous birth to the Czechs thousands of years later desiring to no longer see darker Roma faces in their streets—to be a community of values. This is a wrongful claim: in the absence of choice and in a context where the unilateral totalitarian status assignment—by definition value-blind—prevails, the preservation of a community of values argument amounts to the glorification of the randomness of the distribution of the status, nothing else.

In fact, were it indeed truly random, it would already be a very positively biased picture, since, as we have seen in the chapters on the status, rights, and duties of citizenship, these are all usually used to discriminate and exclude *particular* groups. Preserving and reinforcing sex discrimination and racism have traditionally been the primary functions of citizenship, not merely occasional deviations from some kind of an equal ideal. Branding the Roma in the Czech Republic as "Slovaks" is not a random act, just like any other decision on who is to belong to the "real community" in the society a person lives in. Indeed, none of the status deprivations are random, or necessarily connected to whatever their official justifications may be. The emphasis is usually laid on the need "to respect the law", which is obviously written from a citizenship—meaning, exclusion—perspective—that has traditionally been sexist and racist on one side and nationalist on the other. When a U.S. ICE officer—a servant of the people of the only country you know and grew up in, as with the DACA youth—tells you that you "do not belong" and should be deported, this is not a random act, it is the violence citizenship is precisely *designed* for, again justified by the myth of values and the morgana castle of self-determination: a self-serving legal fiction. Your values—either overlapping with the ones proclaimed by the state deporting you, or not—do not matter at all. What matters is that you are proclaimed a "foreigner" and served with a deportation order.

That said, a truly random distribution of rights can be a value to stand by; that was how some ancient Greek polities would select their officials from the citizenry. Bearing this in mind, we can safely agree that excluding others, even residents from birth, from the status of citizenship for the sake of preserving a truly random assignment of political rights would obviously make no sense at all. In fact, it goes against the very idea of liberty that political rights are there to forge. Once again, the fact that we know that the distribution is in fact not random does not make this failing argument any stronger. As an instrument of closure justified by the need to preserve a certain system of values, citizenship makes no logical sense. Notwithstanding the obvious flaws of the political self-determination argument, it has appealed to scholars and statesmen in helping delimit the body of citizens, to create a seemingly sound basis for the creation of foreigners and aliens open to being denied their claim to be "free."

Politics and Citizenship Correlation

Two trends in the development of political rights shed light on how the self-determination argument underlying the connection between citizenship status and political rights lost its traction.

The first key trend behind the development of political rights is co-directional with the general trend in the politics of citizenship over roughly the last hundred years, which is two-dimensional. On the one hand, increasing numbers of resident minorities have acquired the right to citizenships that are less totalitarian and more attentive to the situation on the ground in the actual society, with its diversity and idiosyncrasies. So "Turks" can now naturalize in Germany, although it is more difficult for them to do than for the occasional Pole, Frenchman, or Irishman, as they remain second-rate compared with "Europeans" in German naturalization law. The Chinese and the Japanese, previously excluded on grounds of race, can now naturalize in the United States. Naturalization means entitlement to political participation.

Furthermore, on the other hand, a growing number of individuals who hold the formal legal status of citizenship can actually use political rights. As we have seen in chapter 4, the narrative of duties no longer acts to justify the total exclusion of women from political rights, and minorities are also enfranchised in many places around the world as long as they hold citizenship. There has thus been a glorious march forward of political rights. Indeed, were "self-determination" and "freedom" to become convincing, enlarging the numbers of those who participate is a logical direction to take. At the same time, given that citizenship as a status of random exclusion relies extensively on the mythology of values underlying the political community, the link between the need to possess the status and the right to vote generally remains unbroken, even though the absurdity of regarding citizenship as a litmus test of commitment—let alone full-hearted membership—in a political community is self-evident, as the accounts of all the "bad" citizens illustrate. All the Brodskys, Einsteins, deserters, hippies, and Holocaust deniers come to mind. This obvious point is illustrated well by the discrepancy between the number of citizens and the actual turnout rates at elections, where there are elections at all, as shown for the sample of countries in figure 7.

In other words, the first trend in the area of political rights ensures that more previously excluded groups can enjoy the full rights of citizenship, but stops short of the ultimate logical outcome of the trend that reigns, as we have seen, in civil and social rights and to a limited degree the right to be present in the country. The status of citizenship in the area of the political has not been decoupled from the enjoyment of rights: the march is glorious up to a point. The implications of this are far-reaching and far more important than determining who will cast a vote for the Gibraltar assembly, the Viennese mayor, the Scottish parliament, or in the U.S. presidential elections.

Indeed, the actual composition of voter rolls recedes as a factor in comparison to the dramatic impact the rationales of political enfranchisement have on access to the *status* of citizenship. Such rationales ensure that many members of society are excluded from this status and the rights it brings in the name of the "political self-determination" of a different group in the same society, as we have seen with the Roma, who should all be from Slovakia, if the Nazi reports on the successes of the holocaust in the Czech lands are presumed to be correct. Duties have traditionally been rhetorically deployed against women to ensure that they are excluded from political rights while formally included in citizenship status. The exclusion of old and new resident ethnic minorities from citizenship is usually rhetorically justified by "democracy," not "duties." This is what Michael Walzer referred to as the emergence of "citizen-tyrants."[10] An illustration of this is the traditionally harsh exclusion of Germans of Turkish origin from citizenship, which is still the practice in the country, ensuring the presence of millions of permanent residents unable to participate in politics and thus unable to be "free."[11] Different naturalization rules apply to "Turks" and "Europeans." It is not the denial of political rights, however, that is the biggest problem for minorities such as this; it is the denial or complication of access to the very status of citizenship with all the other rights that flow from it that is critical, especially the right to reside and work in the country. This occurs in the name of "protecting" the political community, through ensuring that neighbors and fellow members of the society who are discriminated against remain in a profoundly subjugated position in the interest of continued discrimination—in other words, "citizenship." "Citizen-tyrants" are thus arch-enemies of Robert Dahl's "principle of affected interests,"[12] which entails allowing those who are most affected by the laws to have a say.

Latvia and Estonia offer a more radical example in their bizarre practice of forging ethnic electorates after the re-emergence of the two republics from years of Soviet occupation:[13] "Russian speakers" are not entitled to vote in national elections and citizenship is not easily available. To acquire political rights, these minorities are offered a humiliating procedure for naturalizing in their own country, just like American Samoans in the United States,[14] representatives of "non-titular" ethnic groups in Myanmar,[15] or the Turkish minority in Germany at a certain point. Unsurprisingly, the numbers of those willing to go through the ritual, which is designed to punish them by association for the sins of a country that no longer exists and where many of them have never lived (or been), are not high.[16] An interesting situation emerges: citizenship and its core rights are denied to minority members of the society based on arguments of the "democratic self-determination" of the majority, which perpetuates its dominance and enhances the vulnerability and exclusion of the subjugated residents. This is a textbook example of how citizenship always operates in practice, or else the status as such would not be necessary.

Given that the distinction between the society of settled residents and the political community is obviously flawed in a context where governance is territorial and democracies, ideally, are not tribal, connecting the possession of citizenship status and voting is a justification of a profoundly divisive outcome that can only please those willing to look down on minorities and foreigners, as many people of course are, which explains the persistent practice. Theorists of both liberal and communitarian inclinations generally seem, surprisingly, to be eagerly complicit with the key claim of the citizenship/political community connection, as Heather Lardy, among others, has shown.[17] The main problem in this context with arguments for preservation of the democratic community is that they rephrase racism and other sins, presenting them in apparently noble terms. We hear about "culture," "values," and "intergenerational interests," but not about the two key assumptions: political loyalty and the engagement of citizens as opposed to residents, and the genuinely transformative effects of naturalizations on the admitted foreigners. Walzer is right in stating that it is not the minorities, ultimately, but the democratic principles and legitimacy of the government as such that suffer as a result of the application of the now-dominant approach. There is obviously no democracy in Narva, to return to one of the earlier examples, and there never has been, unfortunately. As long as democracies are tribal, the integration of minorities is obviously a very difficult matter: liberal democratic ideals cannot depend on accents and skin pigmentation. As long as they do, citizenship, as the main tool of exclusion from political rights, will continue to be a very effective and powerful instrument of oppression.

Tribalism: Deterritorialization of the Political

The second key trend undermining the political self-determination mythology is even more telling. The re-ethnicization of citizenship in recent decades coupled with the rise in the toleration of the cumulation of nationalities has led to the emergence in the context of numerous citizenships of vast diasporas of status holders abroad. When this reality first emerged, states policed political rights by excluding non-resident citizens from their enjoyment. The connection between the political community and the territory where the laws it sanctions apply is the starting point of thinking about self-governance. It is not surprising in this context that leaving the territory weakens the link with one's political brethren, as the story goes. In the telling 1976 case of *X v. UK* illustrating this, the European

Commission for Human Rights—the predecessor of the European Court of Human Rights in Strasbourg—found no violation in the disenfranchisement of UK citizens working for the European Union (the European Communities at the time) in Brussels, and summarized the reasons for the then-recent general practice of disenfranchising citizens who chose to live abroad as follows:

> First, the assumption that a non-resident citizen
> is less directly or continuously concerned with and
> has less knowledge of its day-to-day problems;
> secondly, the impracticability for and sometimes
> undesirability (in some cases impossibility) of
> Parliamentary candidates of presenting the
> different electoral issues to citizens abroad so as
> to secure a free expression of opinion; thirdly, the
> influence of resident non-citizens on the selection of
> candidates and on the formulation of their electoral
> programmes; and finally, the correlation between
> one's right to vote in Parliamentary elections and
> being directly affected by acts of the political bodies
> so elected.[18]

Britons departing for their own overseas territories or abroad still lose their right to vote for the Westminster Parliament after fifteen years of residence outside the UK, no matter whether they are in Brussels, Bermuda, or South Sudan. This vision, effectively making political rights territorial, was only logical in the context of the main assumption that the "political community" of citizens is value-laden and territorially self-governing. In fact, the importance of territory predictably seemed to be such that some countries would weaken the requirement for possession of citizenship status for the enjoyment of political rights, as long as the residence in the territory box was checked. The UK, which still partly follows this approach, grants full political rights in its territory to all the legally resident nationals of the Commonwealth of Nations or the Irish—its old colonial club.[19] Historically, such enactments of "no taxation without representation" logic were also accepted in the United States, where all those who filed a declaration of their intent to naturalize acquired active political rights on par with U.S. citizens, until the spike in nationalism of World War I.[20]

The vision of the European Commission for Human Rights, notwithstanding all the arguments in its favor, does *not* reflect the state of play in the domain of citizens' enfranchisement around the world today. As we have seen, the political rights of citizenship, while still essentially connected to the possession of the status, are now divorced from residence considerations in all key jurisdictions that hold elections, from the United States, France, India, Italy, Japan, and Namibia to Russia and Singapore. A great deal has changed since 1976. Rainer Bauböck is correct in his analysis of this aspect of the citizenship and rights correlation, describing the political rights of expatriate citizens as "contingently legitimate."[21] In the end, all the arguments for and against considered, states prefer to not allow residence considerations to alter the scope of citizens' political rights, as empirical research shows—more than a hundred countries currently allow for one of the many forms of expatriate voting from abroad.[22] This is a very large number, considering that half the world's nations—slightly under a hundred—are not democracies and either do not hold elections at all, or hold elections deprived of any relevance.[23]

The reasons behind the enfranchisement of nonresident citizens are difficult to contest. Even if not subjected to most laws of the country where they do not reside, citizens depend—by virtue of their very legal existence—on the citizenship law of their country, and often on other matters, such as taxation and diplomatic protection. More importantly, the international agreements and alliances of the country of citizenship, which are sometimes put to a referendum, can have overwhelming immediate importance for the scope of rights and obligations of the expatriate citizens. Brexit is the best example here: those UK citizens who benefited from the European Union the most, having settled on the continent using their EU-law intercitizenship—the right to choose the country of residence of their liking—were precisely those who could not vote in the referendum on leaving the EU in June 2015, or at least, not the 700,000[24] who had stayed on the continent fifteen years or more. As a result of the vote, their rights to live, work, and to not be discriminated against as Britons in the European Union will expire without their having had any say whatsoever. In the case of Brexit, the expatriate voting that many UK citizens were not able to enjoy could well have been a game changer.[25]

It is not surprising, therefore, that in recent decades the paradigm of the territoriality of the political has been entirely reversed in the national elections around the world: instead of enfranchising some residents without citizenship and disenfranchising non-resident citizens, the majority of states where elections at least nominally matter now do precisely the opposite: citizens retain the vote no matter where they decide to reside, while residents without citizenship are disenfranchised. Political rights are no longer purely territorial. Polish politicians campaign in London and Ireland, where hundreds of thousands of voters live. The senator for French citizens abroad visits her constituents in Dubai and Bahrain. Turkish ministers rely on their expats to deepen the assault on democracy in Ankara and consider it their right to rally crowds of Turks in The Hague and Berlin. They are surprised to be asked to leave the Netherlands, calling Dutch democracy a "Nazi remnant."[26] It is not the enfranchisement of the expats, who would then actively help install a dictatorship "back home" where they do not live, however, that is the core of the problem, but the non-extension of political rights to non-citizen residents, who make up the social reality of any state's society.

Current developments do not change the basic element of territoriality underlying governance. Given that the scope of the majority of legal rules around the world is still territorial, the tyranny Michael Walzer spoke about has now principally doubled in nature: a non-resident citizen not subjected to the majority of the laws of the country and probably never having visited the site where her political community reigns will now decide who will be making the rules to govern all the aspects of the lives of resident non-citizens, who do not themselves have a right to vote (but might be entitled to elect the rulers of their own legal "home" far away to govern its remote inhabitants). Moreover, the enfranchisement of expats, which comes about in tandem with the strict exclusion of non-citizen residents from political rights, obviously provides a huge challenge to the core ideology of the political community and the bounded nation-state that brings it to life via citizenship laws.

Residence and citizenship rights can be particularly blurred in colonial and postcolonial contexts. Ugly in-between examples are thus possible: under Dutch rules, the Dutch anywhere in the world could participate in national and European elections unless they choose to reside in the (now-reformed) colonies, since while Dutch voters who live anywhere else in the world "still have links with the Netherlands society,"[27] those who move to Aruba or Curaçao are presumed by the Dutch government to have lost such ties. A former colony still forming part of the Kingdom of the Netherlands is thus radically different in Dutch law from Melbourne or Portland—and from Amsterdam to Delft as well. The colonies have their own assemblies, you see,[28] even though plenty of crucial decisions—the legislation on citizenship, for instance, which can be steeply discriminatory against the Caribbean parts of the Dutch Kingdom[29]—are taken by the Dutch parliament in The Hague, not in the colonial city of Oranjestad off the northern coast of Venezuela.

While the Dutch colonial example is an attempt to turn the Kingdom's overseas territories into political non-spaces carved out from the face of the Earth— what the absolute majority of colonies have always been by definition—bigger questions about the meaning of residence emerge in numerous countries. The world has moved on from palaces and castles as the determinants of wealth and power to private jets and the possession of a passport that opens doors: a modern global leader will many times more likely be a Norwegian than a Pakistani citizen, to return to the example we started with. A global leader simply cannot be locked in a low-HDI country where the likelihood of economic success, per Milanovic, is incomparably lower than elsewhere, holding a substandard passport that makes travel extremely difficult and relocation to another country virtually impossible, unless you are a refugee. However rich and well-educated you are, once a Pakistani, the removal of the glass ceiling of that nationality is indispensable for global success.[30] Dozens of other countries could be used as an example here instead of Pakistan. Harpaz refers to the need to upgrade one's nationality, which is clear even if there is no intent to migrate, as seeking a "compensatory citizenship."[31] As people become more itinerant, residence shifts from being a crystal-clear concept resulting from habitual grounding of a life in a particular community into a legal fiction similar to citizenship, a legal status attested to by a residence permit, municipal registration, and the authority taxing you. Indeed, it can also be negative: under tax residence arrangements of a number of countries the resident brings an oath not to reside for half a year in every tax year in any jurisdiction in the world, while having no obligation to do that in the country offering the service and collecting (a significantly lower) tax the "negative" resident pays. To get a discount one needs to move. The fluidity of contemporary residence as such undermines the clarity of the boundaries the world of citizenship rests upon, with implications for its legitimacy, territoriality, and governance.[32]

An important lesson emerges. Notwithstanding the fact that governance is territorial, territoriality is *no longer* a crucial element of the construction of political rights and neither is residence—unless a Dutchman moves from pretty much anywhere in the world to colorful Oranjestad. Only citizenship is crucial now—and it has not been in such a monopoly position before, as we have seen. Coupled with the blurring of the meaning of residence as such, the consequences of this development for the persuasiveness of the narrative of collective self-determination are drastic: democracy becomes tribal while the legal systems remain territorial. With the increase in the scale of migration around the world, the disconnect between citizenship tribalism and territorial legalism is bound only to grow, undermining the main product of a functioning democracy: the legitimacy of government among those subjected to its authority.

Some countries, such as France and Portugal, recognize the far-reaching implications of such developments, mitigating the possible negative outcomes.[33] Co-nationals abroad are represented via special seats in their legislatures, establishing a clear quota and allowing them to lobby for their rights via their own pool of representatives in the legislature. Italy, Hungary, and the United States provide the contrary examples: without special representation quotas and seats in the legislature, co-nationals abroad can both directly affect the outcome of national elections and do *not* have their specific overseas interests represented.

This is precisely why Prime Minister Berlusconi decided to enfranchise all the hundreds of thousands of Italians abroad, whom Italy had created as Italians since the citizenship law reform of 1992, and why Prime Minister Orbán made half a million Hungarians in Serbia, Ukraine, Slovakia, and Romania in the wake of his reelection in 2014. Some mass naturalizations are done specifically to grant the right to vote. For Berlusconi it was a misjudgment: foreign Italians brought Prodi to power in 2006,[34] while Orbán was wiser: the votes of the new Hungarians in the former "greater Hungary" have proven crucial to retaining his constitutional majority and continuing the dismantling of the rule of law in the ailing EU state.[35]

The United States stands as a worrisome illustration of the second aspect of the two we outlined: while theoretically affecting the national electoral outcomes, the expats do *not* have their specific overseas interests represented. Without own congressmen and senators, as is the case of expats in France, Portugal, and many other nations, Americans abroad are de facto left without a way to influence their government via elections, subjected to nothing but a tyranny of the majority: The 2010 Foreign Account Tax Compliance Act, or FATCA, aiming to clamp down on tax evasion, created such reporting burdens on foreign banks that the lives of ordinary U.S. citizen expats have come to be negatively affected.[36] Given that different rules now apply to the accounts held outside of the United States by

Americans compared with the citizens of all the other nations, holding U.S. citizenship abroad has abruptly become very costly for Americans of every income level, affecting both the rich and the poor and allowing talk of "citizenship overreach."[37] The billboards of select banks in Zürich now boast, "We even accept Americans!" Renunciations of U.S. citizenship have spiked.[38] Although able to vote, US expats are deprived of the representation of their specific interests on Capitol Hill and clearly suffer as a result.

The Politics of Naturalization

The professed disconnect between a society and a political community as well as the deployment of citizenship to make this divide harsher in the name of democracy obviously casts a shadow over the contemporary idea of naturalization, which now turns a resident into a citizen, admitting him into the body politic. Dora Kostakopoulou's surprised "why naturalisation?" is the most relevant question in this context.[39] Indeed, what are the problems that naturalizations solve compared with the problems they create? The rite of passage for settled foreigners who are already objectively a part of the society, having spent years in the country before submitting their naturalization application documents, only confers the status of citizenship and has nothing to do with actually belonging to the community, besides the reinforced protection from deportation it usually grants. In a situation where the majority of the rights that were previously associated with citizenship are clearly residence-based today, naturalization is usually responsible for the acquisition of one set of rights, the political rights of citizenship, alongside granting unlimited access to the territory. Since being deprived of these rights undermines the legitimacy of the public authorities—turning any democratic claim into a Narva or Qatar reality of tyranny—it cannot be a legitimate aspiration for any government that chose a liberal-democratic route to legitimize itself.

Consequently—and given that citizenship is not about values and is being divorced from territoriality—relying on naturalization for the extension of political rights, although this is prevailing global practice, hardly withstands basic criticism. This is particularly the case in the most mature liberal democratic systems, where the forging of the "good citizen" through the duties of uniformity and complacency is no longer among the main goals of the state. Consequently, naturalization cannot be based—no matter what the official documents claim—on the forging of thick identities and beliefs. Creating "good citizens" was probably the core consideration on which the reasoning behind naturalizations rested, which necessarily came with the presumption that any foreigner is by definition unworthy of inclusion and his barbarianism requires radical cleansing, which naturalization purported to provide. In the current citizenship context, however, rights and non-territorial political empowerment combined with tolerance and at least respect on paper for citizens, as opposed to the objective of breaking them, render naturalization an act devoid of any identifiable meaning, beyond the perpetuation of the logic of exclusion itself.

Naturalization's only significance remains the symbolic glorification of citizenship and the repetition of the litany of citizenship's "values," "duties," and the "defence of the political community," which are all of "second freshness" should we tap into the language of Bulgakov's diabolic cat, the Behemoth. The prevailing practice of connecting political rights and the status of citizenship renders resident minority populations precarious and potentially liable to deportation while also signalling their presumed and inescapable second-rate humanity to all through the denial of political rights to them.

I am not mentioning the arguments of "deserving a citizenship" or "being well prepared for a life in a community," since the overwhelming majority of those naturalizing have already spent years in their adoptive country before applying for citizenship and thus do not need any preparation or enforcement of their linguistic, entrepreneurial, or other skills, even if we believe that this could be a defensible starting point. Even more problematic is the innate assumption that one naturalizes to reside, which is obviously not true, when applied to all the compensatory citizenships as Harpaz explained: one often naturalizes to be Maltese, or American, not to reside in those places, preferring to return to China, Russia, or Israel. And of course we cannot speak of deserving a status, which is per se deprived of dignity and any moral value in a world where its distribution is random. Thinking in these two directions is thus obviously flawed and unpersuasive. Christian Joppke's criticism of this turn is even simpler: "The thrust of liberalization was to turn citizenship into a right, which was paradoxical, because to have rights cannot itself be a right"[40]—or be "deserved" for that matter.

In a world where the majority of the rights previously exclusively reserved for citizenship is now extended to residents, and where citizenship is no longer as violent and intolerant as it used to be, naturalization, the act of policing the citizenship status border, as opposed to the immigration regime granting access to a territory, only makes sense if it is justified by a very important ideal. Ethnic purity or cultural superiority no longer justify, and almost no one would openly glorify the obvious neo-feudal randomness, although this sometimes still happens among the holders of the elite super-citizenships.[41] Consequently, the notion of a "political community" with its "values" is the last bastion justifying citizenship's grip on our imagination. However dull and unconvincing, there is nothing better.

The notion of a "political community" with its "values" is the last bastion justifying citizenship's grip on our imagination. However dull and unconvincing, there is nothing better.

Citizenship without Democracy

Given that political equality among citizens does not extend beyond the one-person, one-vote rule at the ballot box, contemporary citizenship—especially the citizenships that come without rights, only with liabilities—ironically is *not at all political* on its own terms in a huge number of jurisdictions, in contrast to the countless popular claims. Of course there is lobbying, philanthropy, writing op-eds, donating to influential NGOs steering public opinion, research—all this is outside the realm of citizenship's political equality, however. Voting, to which political equality purports to apply in contemporary democracies, is but a drop in the sea of the fundamental ways to influence democratic outcomes, even if the most visible one, as John Mueller has explained.[42] This is good news for non-citizens: a rich world of political activity outside the act of voting per se does not fall within the realm of citizenship-based exclusion.

So while "values" are nowhere in sight in the communities based on strict assignment of belonging from birth, and democratic legitimacy is usually connected to granting the population a formal voice in governing the territory, it is clear that the mythical "body politic," the collective of the self-governing citizens who are "free," is less and less territorial. The voice is heard from abroad, while, at the same time, actual governance is not necessarily dependent as much on voting as the "free" are made to believe. We thus witness a double paradox marking citizenship's raison d'être and key justification.

How important is this growing disconnect between the territory and the political community for the broader picture of citizenship and political rights in the world? Putting the preceding discussion into broader perspective, "The Economist Intelligence Unit's Democracy Index" shows that only 11.4 percent of countries (together inhabited by 4.5 percent of the population of the planet) are "Full Democracies." Even including the 34.1 percent of the countries characterized as "Flawed Democracies" in the count, 54.5 percent of the world's countries lie beyond the democratic realm, making the whole political exclusion rationale absolutely inapplicable per se to the other 50.7 percent of the world's population, inhabiting almost a hundred nations.[43] This situation is not volatile: this reality is with us to stay. Worse still, the number of democracies in the world, as of late, has been falling steadily.

The random exclusion lines surrounding the majority of citizenships worldwide have thus nothing to do with self-determination at all—only with subjugation. The banal violence will usually come—from Iran to Saudi Arabia and Venezuela—with numerous "value"-based claims. The outright absurdity of such claims cannot affect the effectiveness of the citizenship in place in such countries: it ascribes the status of belonging and strictly excludes in the same way that the citizenships in the established democracies do, whether India, the United States, or San Marino. This is why this book did not start, in contrast to the majority of the accounts of citizenship, with the story of political rights. Distinguishing actual functions from their official justifications is of essential importance.

Beyond the half of the world that boasts official citizenship without democracy, turnout at elections is decreasing all around.[44] Throughout the most highly developed countries, the HDI leaders of the world, the appeal of politics as a ballot-box exercise seems to be particularly in decline (figure 8). We should not interpret this decline necessarily negatively, however. Good politics in a well-functioning country—take the Netherlands as an example—is by definition incapable of producing either circus-like fascination or radical change, since there is no winner-takes-all outcome to attract attention. Boredom seems to be the key ingredient of a mature political system. It might take more than two hundred days to get a government in place, at which point the minister president cycles to the king (a nominal but polite figure), the new government is inaugurated, and everything more or less remains the same. In such a situation the decline in the number of voters could also reflect the liberal values of the people making an individual decision to assess their investment in politics more critically, as opposed to a failure of the democratic culture. It is impossible to educate this away:

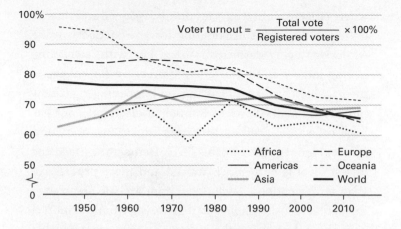

Figure 8 The global decline of voter turnout since World War II
Source: IDEA Voter Turnout Database, www.idea.int/data-tools/data/voter
-turnout, as reported in A. Solijonov, *Voter Turnout Trends around the World*
(Stockholm: IDEA, 2017), 23.
Note: The data is for lower house legislative elections across the globe since
1945, including 1,833 elections in total.

liking elections—besides being irrelevant outside the context of the small share of the world where elections actually matter—cannot be a condition for the enjoyment of citizenship, let alone the core part of its definition.

As we have discussed, the strong link between citizenship and political rights as opposed to residence and political rights—no matter which citizenship you hold—is a development that is contrary to the dynamics of all other citizenship rights. Consequently, radical changes in this area should be expected, especially given that in a world where citizenship status is randomly assigned and thus by definition incapable of standing for any particular value, while also being de-territorialized but with lawmaking having largely territorial effects, pressure for change is inescapable. Such change is indeed happening right now, but mostly at the level of municipal elections—our garbage collection, licenses for street musicians, and snow removal are regulated at this level. Democratic life at the lowest level is both more archaic and more progressive than at the national level. It is more archaic because going abroad usually implies deregistering from the municipality and thus losing the right to vote, no matter what citizenship you hold, confining the body politic to those residing in the municipality. It is progressive, since in plenty of countries citizenship is not a relevant consideration to qualify for the local vote—residence is. Different levels of political belonging imply different strategies for the acquisition of political rights, yet the essential normative reasons behind these differences are not obvious at all. The process of enfranchising foreigners at the local level has not always been smooth—the German Federal Constitutional Court even ruled it impossible once in a nationalist swan song, only to step back after the constitution was changed in response.[45] The absurd argument that you need to be proclaimed to belong to the sacred community of citizens to decide on the garbage removal from your street has ceased to be convincing in Germany. From

Sweden to New Zealand (but not yet in the United States, unlike in the past[46]), participation in local elections no longer is based on citizenship, and this is only the beginning, given the key trends in the area of political rights around the world today already outlined. Moreover, a spillover of more liberal visions of entitlement to participation in national elections is definitely on the agenda, even if it takes a hundred years or more, as did the enfranchisement of women. However slow, it seems to be a logical necessity, if the logic of the body politic is to remain convincing and meaningful.

The growth of intercitizenships is a factor to add to this account: as citizenships increasingly come with virtually unconditional entitlements to build a life in a number of foreign jurisdictions. However, making political rights in the country where you choose to live the price for the use of the rights that intercitizenships grant neither enhances the legitimacy of any government nor increases any value any citizenship would want to protect. It works like this: intercitizenship arrangements, providing virtually unconditional access to work and residence to other nations, do not usually cover political rights. As a result, moving to a different state while using a right of access to that state's territory conferred by your own citizenship—say, settling in Russia with a Belarusian passport, or in France with a Swiss one—does not confer any political rights at the national level in the new state of residence. The absurdity of the classical "he is not a citizen" argument in such context is self-evident.

Timid moves in the direction of enfranchising resident non-citizens can be observed around the world.[47] New Zealand, the absolute leader in this field, allows any permanent resident to vote in the national parliament elections.[48] The UK goes further with the rights granted to the resident citizens of Ireland or the Commonwealth: they not only vote, but they also can run for office. Latin American nations offer easy access to naturalization to neighbors from the same continent, who can thereby acquire full political rights within two years, as Diego Acosta Arcarazo has described. Moving at the highest continental level of politics, the EU Parliament elections are open in terms of passive and active political rights to all EU citizens—nationals of the twenty-eight EU member states—and are exercised without discrimination based on which nationality an individual actually possesses and where in the Union she resides.[49] Daniel Cohn-Bendit, the hero of the 1968 revolution in the streets of Paris, claiming a right denied by puritan French bureaucracy to access the female dormitories of the Sorbonne and thus not be lonely at night,[50] was the first person to benefit from this right: a de jure German representing the people of France in Brussels and Strasbourg. Although these are not national elections, this is still a good start.

SUPER-CITIZENSHIPS

Randomness and Hypocrisy Are Here to Stay

Citizenship is a very unlikely concept to glorify: its only purpose is to divide the world and appear unquestionable and "natural" in the face of the most obvious criticism, rendering states better governable by promoting servility and complacency in the patriotic populations, in democracies and autocracies alike. Its distribution around the world is entirely random and totalitarian: one is a citizen purely on the strength of having been assigned to a particular citizenship by an authority—an authority that brooks no dissent, should you claim to not belong. Your agreement is not necessary and your protests are of no avail, yet everything about you—from life expectancy to your income and basic freedoms inside and outside the assigning state the world over—is in direct correlation with this congenital assignment, in which you can neither participate nor refuse in the majority of cases. The assignment of citizenship is entirely beyond our control and glorified as logical and "natural," yet citizenship is not a force of nature: it is designed with certain groups and people in mind, making sure that those who are disliked or regarded as of little use by the relevant authority at any given moment and for whatever reason will surely be kept down at the time of the initial assignment or later. No protests are expected or tolerated: what is "natural" must be accepted.

Given the radical differences in quality between different citizenships around the world—some bringing amazing rights, others merely poisonous liabilities—the randomized totalitarian assignment endows citizenship with its core function: the preservation of global inequality. Distributed like prizes in a lottery where four-fifths of the world's population loses, citizenship is clothed in the language of self-determination and freedom, elevating hypocrisy as one of the status's core features. Even considering the truly minuscule proportion of the world's population that ever changes its citizenship, the grip of citizenship on our lives is close to absolute, even if it is at times unnoticed. Citizenship's connection to "freedom" and "self-determination" usually stops making any sense at the boundaries of the most affluent Western states. Citizenship, for most of the world's population, is thus an empty rhetorical shell deployed to perpetuate abuse, dispossession, and exclusion. It is a means of directing former colonials to their unenviable place, spiced with a delightfully attractive hint of nationalism.

The glorified "citizenship" of the political science textbooks, bound up with dignity and rights, could not be further disconnected from the citizenship experienced by the majority of the Earth's population, delivering violent liabilities and limiting opportunities: an extinguisher of hope. Citizenship, as one of the key tools for locking the poorest populations within the confines of their dysfunctional states, thus perpetuates and reinforces global inequality, making talk of equality difficult to sustain with a straight face, and denying individual agency through its appeal to a "natural" distribution of lifetime opportunities not open to contestation. Upon critical reflection, the glorified concept boils down to a cocktail of punishing randomness and hypocrisy: two of citizenship's key features, noble justifications aside.

The core business model of this concept has been the extraction of duties from those proclaimed "to belong" in exchange for a state protection racket and associated favors that they can neither choose nor refuse. As a tool for instilling complacency and homogeneity in societies, citizenship has played a key role in silencing dissent and streamlining obedience. Yet it is still generally perceived very positively: citizenship is proclaimed to be magically endowed with "dignity," "values," and "freedom" from

Upon critical reflection, the glorified concept boils down to a cocktail of punishing randomness and hypocrisy: two of citizenship's key features, noble justifications aside.

Kyrgyzstan and Cambodia to Canada and Chad. It is a splendid governance tool that teaches us to ignore the plight of those who have not been assigned the same status at birth as us—a way to justify switching off reason. It is, therefore, crudely nationalist in essence. Yet because of rather than despite all of the above, citizenship occupies a central role in the contemporary world, which is still the world of states, and scholars and politicians compete in offering rationalizing and glorifying accounts of the concept. Citizenship captures our imagination and a good citizen always is said to be ready to die for the values the status installs and preserves.

The preceding chapters have demonstrated that citizenship's positive image has little to do with the reality on the ground and the causes of this deep disconnect are not difficult to uncover. Long overdue is criticism of the liberal nationalist traditions inspiring the popular visions of citizenship today—either explicitly or implicitly. As we have seen, discussion of citizenship as a positive force is impossible outside of a dreamworld where every nation is set in a vast expanse of nothingness. It is fundamental to focus on citizenship's essential, built-in chronic pathologies, which this book has outlined, in order to start a nuanced debate on the possible place that citizenship could occupy in the world of tomorrow. The gulf between the notion of citizenship and the positive, glorifying narrative surrounding it has never been wider than today. This gulf has never been more undeniable, either. All those desiring to restore citizenship to some mythic historical ideal—a huge trend in contemporary literature—are never open about the simple fact that there is nothing to restore, unless they feel like returning to colonialism and strict observance of racist and sexist rules imposed territorially by belligerent societies demanding enormous sacrifices from those who are proclaimed to belong, total submission from those who are not, and tolerating no dissent. Where citizenship is assessed critically, approached through an empirically informed global perspective—rather than a purely normative, one-nation lens blind to the harms the concept has been *designed* to inflict—there is no place for giving it any undeserved credit for its mythical "value." Instead, the injustice, the pain, and the arbitrary servile violence inherent in citizenship are bound to be noticed, recorded, and analyzed.

The most frequent mistake in approaching citizenship, however, is not related to its inexplicable glorification. It is ignoring the importance of the legal status at the heart of this concept. Underplaying it misrepresents all the essential characteristics of citizenship entirely. Once the status and the rules for its assignment are placed at the center of the citizenship story, the multitude of citizenships around the world and the strict boundaries between them naturally become the focal point of discussion, making myopic confocal misrepresentations like T.H. Marshall's very difficult, if not impossible.

This is the context in which we suddenly become able to discover that citizenship is under tremendous pressure, which could in theory endanger the concept's very survival. Contemporary law and politics are built on the ethical base of equal human worth and the idea of deserving and achievement: the world has officially moved far away from the caste structures of the past: children in every school are taught to realize their potential by studying hard and taking control of their future into their own hands. The core idea of fairness informing the contemporary understanding of law and politics is inspired by Enlightenment reason and is centered on the belief that the individual is in charge and the authority is able and willing to back its decisions with recourse to valid reasons and clear arguments. Tragically for citizenship, any appeal to this concept is nothing but shorthand for the denial of all such foundational positions. Worse still, adapting its essence so that contemporary fairness can be incorporated into the story of citizenship is absolutely impossible. Citizenship *is precisely about* mass caste assignments in a context where individual agency and all the personal characteristics of the bearers are dismissed by definition. It is an abstract totalitarian status struggling to survive in a world where all it has ever cherished and promoted is untenable in principle even if it survives in practice, once it is taken beyond the context of a particular group endowed with the same status. As the realization of this simple fact grows, the prestige of citizenship is bound to diminish very steeply. In the contemporary world of reasoning rooted in globally shared understandings—such as equal human worth, agency, and fairness, for instance—a status boasting no compelling rationale on its side beyond simple convenience of the preservation of the status quo—"are you really arguing for bringing down that wall?"—will struggle to survive, and thus is bound, sooner or later, to follow its own foundational features, which are no longer there: sexism, racism, and the intolerance of individuality outside the officially mandated litanies of "good citizenship." Because in reality our world is not arbitrary and not totalitarian in its ideals, it therefore is not an ideal foundation for classical citizenship: all the hypocrisy in the world will not be enough to misrepresent current cultural and legal developments in a citizenship-friendly vein: the good ship *Citizenship* is sinking with all its glorious though very dated music playing on board, and only nationalists (liberal—and not so liberal) will be saddened at its loss.

How sudden will this sinking be? It is absolutely clear at this point that citizenship is too much part of the current and constantly employed toolbox used to produce, reproduce, and explain our day-to-day reality. Change will come gradually—and this is what we are already observing the world over. With the global rise of intercitizenships, the correlation between the status and the territory of rights is also broken. Moreover, the granting of political rights to expats in situations where non-citizens at home do not vote undermines the core justification behind citizenship today—political self-determination. Nothing is worse for the status of enabling "self-determination"— citizenship's most routine justification—than making democracies tribal in a global context while governance remains strictly territorial. At the level of rights more generally, citizenship status is being reassessed as a trigger of rights: once scholars have read the Napoleonic Code, the Marshallian misrepresentations of rights do not quite fly, as we have seen. If the citizenship element is becoming increasingly redundant as a proxy for the activation of civil and social rights, at a certain point it also becomes too much of a stretch to claim that it is indispensable for political rights—after all, it is not.

Super-Citizenships

The emerging picture of the citizenship of the near future is that of a legal status, ever more difficult to justify, yet still overwhelmingly important in everyone's life: citizenships grant access to the territory where the protection of rights happens in practice and where life opportunities—either privileged or downgraded—materialize.

Even more, several dozen select super-citizenships—the majority associated with the former empires—elevate their randomly assigned holders to remarkable heights in a world of opportunities, compared with all other citizenship statuses in the world. The nations granting super-citizenships—the EU member states, the United States, and a tiny number of others, the states covering the majority of the map in figure 1—are the economic and democratic leaders of the world. Those empowered by their citizenships perceive citizenship's main function—the creation and policing of arbitrary impenetrable borders—differently from the majority of the world's population. A super-citizenship is not about boundaries, it is about the gates of opportunity. Super-citizenships thus function differently in principle compared to the statuses that the world's mortals—including Brazilians, Israelis, and Indians—receive. A super-citizenship is not a limit, it is a tremendous boost. The gap between the super-citizenships of the world and the other citizenship statuses, which is already huge, is only bound to grow in the future. It will concern all the aspects of life: the general wealth, education, security, and advancements in medicine available to the world's super-citizens will make the gulf between them and others even wider than it is today—the fifty-times difference in the chances of a citizen child dying before reaching the age of five compared with a super-citizen child is only the beginning. Bionics and medical technology will help the super-citizens first. Artificial intelligence and blockchain technology will most likely separate super-citizens even further from the rest, as the policing of the boundary between the world's highest caste and the rest becomes cheaper and more efficient. However thinning and unjustifiable, citizenship has not yet revealed its darkest reaches in full.

In addition to the thinning of citizenship combined with the simultaneous rise of super-citizenships—marked by an ever-increasing gap between the most elite citizenships in the world and all the rest—it is possible to predict the continued contamination of citizenship, with all its totalitarianism and caste mentality, by the contemporary ideals of fairness, universal human worth, and individual justice, as opposed to punishment by association. While reconciliation here is impossible—it would require the abolition of citizenship on the spot, which is nowhere in sight, since the concept is too effective at governing populations and mobilizing complacency—it is possible to expect growing attention to the personal circumstances of all citizens and foreign residents alike. The precursors of this are fast-track super-citizenships for the losers in the birthright lottery who are nonetheless endowed with particular skills, talents, or money: talented sports figures, world-renowned artists and scientists, leading entrepreneurs.

Such individualization is more in tune with the ideals of fairness and merit than the endowment of rigid caste systems with proclaimed dignity, which remains integral to citizenship today. Pushed to the extreme by the absurd rhetoric of citizenship's "values," such points-based citizenship and immigration systems would require removing super-citizenships from the ugly, the poor, the badly educated, and the unsuccessful (as viewed by the issuing authority, of course). As a totalitarian status of absolute domination that is distributed randomly, citizenship is bound to remain in deep opposition to all that we believe about fairness and freedom, in a world where the quality of the statuses a Finn and a Congolese get is incommensurable and the rationalizations for this reality are too esoteric to remain intellectually honest.

However symbolically strong citizenship seems to be, the question of its continued relevance and much needed justification has never been more acute than now, as the core features and effects of citizenship, such as racism, sexism, and randomness disconnected from the holders' desires and merit, can no longer be accepted as possibly legitimate without any critical interrogation. Attempts to succeed within the context of particular societies, with citizenship's key promises of equality, mutual respect, and self-government potentially undermine the essence of citizenship, which is the justification of randomized exclusion, reinforcement of complacency, and the upholding of the status quo. Citizenship thus does not "improve": the result of its evolution can only be the opening of the Pandora's box of interrogating its basic relevance. Citizenship, while still glorified, emerges as entirely unnecessary in a context where its success can no longer be measured by delivering on the ethically and morally repugnant constituents of its essence: if we believe in the ideals it proclaims and apply those globally, citizenship is bound to perish. Once we describe its actual functioning in faithful, accurate terms, it cannot under any circumstances be justified. This is precisely what makes citizenship so fascinating to study: one is compelled to use "values" and "self-determination" to describe a world order where punishing randomness and hypocrisy reign.

ACKNOWLEDGMENTS

This work draws on my teaching on various aspects of citizenship and migration around the world. In particular, *Citizenship* capitalizes on a semester-long conversation with four bright Princeton freshmen in the context of an eponymous Amy Guttmann Seminar in Human Values. Dear Alis, Amma, Olivia, Ryan, I am very grateful to you. Last but not least, I am deeply grateful to Vladimir Bošković, Martijn van den Brink, Aleksejs Dimitrovs, Christian Joppke, Harry Panagopoulos, Suryapratim Roy, Peter Spiro, Kristin Surak, John Torpey, and many other friends who commented on this little book before it went to print. Katie Helke and Kathleen Caruso of MIT Press have been remarkably attentive and helpful editors—and the three anonymous reviewers of the manuscript have done a tremendous job: there are slightly fewer embarrassing mistakes left in the book thanks to them. I am equally grateful to the staff of Rojo's Roastery in Princeton, Fuglen in Oslo, Black and Bloom in Groningen, Augies in Claremont, and all the other cafés where this book was written. I thank Endi Spaho and Jacquelyn Veraldi for excellent research assistance.

TABLE OF CASES

NOTES

Chapter 1

1. The popularly cited figure, which is 2 percent, is probably too optimistic, since the whole bulk of the world's emigrants is estimated by the IOM at about 3.5 percent and not all the emigrants naturalize in their new home. See International Organization for Migration (IOM), *Migration Data Portal* (2017), https://migrationdataportal.org/data?i=stock_abs_origin&t=2017.

2. J. Sater, "Citizenship and Migration in Arab Gulf Monarchies," *Citizenship Studies* 18 (2014): 292. Qatari citizens make up around 10–13 percent of the population of the country: e.g., Z. R. Babar, "The Cost of Belonging: Citizenship Construction in the State of Qatar," *Middle East Journal* 68 (2014): 403.

3. B. Baker, *Estimates of the Unauthorized Immigrant Population Residing in the United States: January 2014*, Population Estimates, Office of Immigration Statistics (July 2017), 4, https://www.dhs.gov/sites/default/files/publications/Unauthorized%20Immigrant%20Population%20Estimates%20in%20the%20US%20January%202014_1.pdf.

4. P. Christiaans and M. Schrover, "Het Oudpaspoortarchief (1950–1959)," in *Bronnen betreffende de registraties van vreemdelingen in Nederland in de negentiende en twintigste eeuw*, ed. M. Schrover (The Hague: Instituut voor Nederlandse Geschiedenis, 2002), 156.

5. J. Zorn, "Non-citizens in Slovenia: Erasure from the Register of Permanent Residents," in *Statelessness in the European Union: Displaced, Undocumented, Unwanted*, ed. C. Sawyer and B. K. Blitz (Cambridge: Cambridge University Press, 2011), 195.

6. UNICEF, "Percentage of Girls and Women Aged 15–49 Years Who Have Undergone FGM (by Place of Residence and Household Wealth Quintile)," UNICEF, February 2018, https://data.unicef.org/wp-content/uploads/2017/11/FGMC-Women-prevalence-database_Oct-2018.xlsx.

7. In Saudi Arabia, beheading is a penalty for exercising freedom of thought and religion, since this is how apostasy is punished: E. Peiffer, "The Death Penalty in Traditional Islamic Law and as Interpreted in Saudi Arabia and Nigeria," *William & Mary Journal of Women and the Law* 11 (2005): 507.

8. On the regime in Turkmenistan, see S. Peyrouse, *Turkmenistan* (London: Routledge, 2015).

9. In *University College London v. Newman* (Westminster County Court, UK, November 7, 1984, para. 7) the judge described the facts as follows: "Since leaving New Zealand the Defendant has become a rather aimless drifter who has spent his time in what is inelegantly but descriptively called colloquially 'bumming' around Europe."

10. A. Shachar, *The Birthright Lottery* (Cambridge, MA: Harvard University Press, 2009).

11. D. Kochenov and J. Lindeboom, eds., *Kälin and Kochenov's Quality of Nationality Index*, 4th ed. (London: Bloomsbury, 2019).

12. C. Stychin, *Governing Sexuality: The Changing Politics of Citizenship and Law Reform* (Oxford: Hart, 2003); B. Cossman, *Sexual Citizens: The Legal and Cultural Regulation of Sex and Belonging* (Stanford, CA: Stanford University Press, 2007).

13. B. Milanovic, *Global Inequality* (Cambridge, MA: Belknap Press of Harvard University, 2016).

14. Ibid., 5.

15. UN Inter-agency Group for Child Mortality Estimation, "Mortality Rate, under-5 (Per 1,000 Live Births)," World Bank (2016), https://data.worldbank.org/indicator/SH.DYN.MORT?year_high_desc=true. There are 95 deaths per 1,000 live births in the first five years of life in the DRC, 54 in the Republic of Congo, and 2 in Finland.

16. Human Development Index is a composite index of life expectancy, education, and per-capita income used by the United Nations Development Programme (UNDP) to assess the country's level of development.

17. D. Kamen, *Status in Classical Athens* (Princeton, NJ: Princeton University Press, 2013), 43–61.

18. *The Economist*, "The Economist Intelligence Unit's Democracy Index" (updated annually), https://www.eiu.com/topic/democracy-index.

19. A. Magen, "The Democratic Entitlement in an Era of Democratic Recession," *Cambridge Journal of International and Comparative Law* 4 (2015): 368.

20. D. Archibugi, *The Global Commonwealth of Citizens* (Princeton, NJ: Princeton University Press, 2008), 24.

21. C. Johnson, "Who Is Aristotle's Citizen?," *Phronesis* 29 (1984): 73–90.

22. C. Joppke, "The Instrumental Turn of Citizenship," *Journal of Ethnic and Migration Studies* 44 (2018), 1. Cf. M. Oakeshott, *On Human Conduct* (Oxford: Oxford University Press, 1975).

23. "Agreement between the European Community and Its Member States, on the one part, and the Swiss Confederation, on the other, on the free

movement of persons" [2002] OJ L114/6; S. Peers, "The EC-Switzerland Agreement on Free Movement of Persons," *European Journal of Migration and Law* 2 (2000): 127.

24. T. H. Marshall, *Class, Citizenship, and Social Development* (Chicago: University of Chicago Press, 1977).

25. L. H. Edmondson, "Was There a Movement for Civil Rights in Russia in 1905?," in *Civil Rights in Imperial Russia*, ed. O. Crisp and L. H. Edmondson (Oxford: Clarendon Press, 1989), 263–286.

26. P. Ismard, *Democracy's Slaves: A Political History of Ancient Greece*, trans. J. M. Todd (Cambridge, MA: Harvard University Press, 2017).

27. L. Siedentop, *Inventing the Individual* (Cambridge, MA: Belknap Press of Harvard University, 2014).

28. E. Cohen, *Semi-Citizenship in Democratic Politics* (Cambridge: Cambridge University Press, 2009).

29. I. Berlin, "Equality," *Proceedings of the Aristotelian Society* 56 (1955–1956): 301, 319.

30. L. P. Pojman, "Are Human Rights Based on Equal Human Worth?," *Philosophy and Phenomenological Research* 52 (1992): 605, 622.

31. Decree of the President of the Republic of Belarus of April 2, 1015, No. 3, "On the Prevention of Social Dependency," http://www.mintrud.gov.by/ru/decret_o_igd/.

32. J. Abrams, "Examining Entrenched Masculinities in the Republican Government Tradition," *West Virginia Law Review* 114 (2011): 165.

33. R. C. Visek, "Creating Ethnic Electorate through Legal Restorationism," *Harvard International Law Journal* 38 (1997): 315.

34. P. Van Elsuwege, *From Soviet Republics to Member States*, 2 vols. (Dordrecht: Martinus Nijhoff, 2008); I. Ziemele, *State Continuity and Nationality* (Dordrecht: Martinus Nijhoff, 2005).

35. P. Weil, *The Sovereign Citizen* (Philadelphia: University of Pennsylvania Press, 2012).

36. For a very good overview of the most popular theories out there, see M. Gibney, "The Rights of Non-citizens to Membership," in *Statelessness in the European Union: Displaced, Undocumented, Unwanted*, ed. C. Sawyer and B. Blitz (Cambridge: Cambridge University Press, 2011), 41. Cf. Z. Oklopcic, *Beyond the People* (Oxford: Oxford University Press, 2018).

37. Archibugi, *The Global Commonwealth of Citizens*, 8.

38. J. Habermas, *The Postnational Constellation*, trans. M. Pensky (Cambridge: Polity, 2001), 1.

39. J. Cadiot, "Searching for Nationality: Statistics and National Categories at the End of the Russian Empire (1897–1917)," *Russian Review* 64 (2005): 440.

40. E. Weber, *Peasants into Frenchmen* (Stanford, CA: Stanford University Press, 1976).

41. B. Anderson, *Imagined Communities: Reflections on the Origin and Spread of Nationalism* (New York: Verso, 1983).

42. P. Szobar, "Telling Sexual Stories in the Nazi Courts of Law," *Journal of the History of Sexuality* 11 (2002): 131, 141.

43. C. Hickman, "The Devil and the One Drop Rule," *Michigan Law Review* 95 (1967): 1161, esp. 1178n72.

44. V. Dominguez, *White by Definition: Social Classification in Creole Louisiana* (New Brunswick, NJ: Rutgers University Press, 1993).

45. P. Bourdieu, "The Force of Law," *Hastings Law Journal* 38 (1987): 835.

46. J. M. Balkin, "The Proliferation of Legal Truth," *Harvard Journal of Law & Public Policy* 26 (2003): 9.

47. B. de Hart, "The Morality of Maria Toet: Gender, Citizenship and the Construction of the Nation State," *Journal of Ethnic and Migration Studies* 32 (2006): 49.

48. De Talavera's father converted, in fact, but the stigma of alienation sometimes does not stop at the generational boundary: A. Feros, *Speaking of Spain* (Cambridge, MA: Harvard University Press, 2017), 83.

49. Siedentop, *Inventing the Individual*.

50. K. Kim, *Aliens in Mediaeval Law* (Cambridge: Cambridge University Press, 2000).

51. F. de Varennes, *Language, Minorities, and Human Rights* (Dordrecht: Kluwer, 1996).

Chapter 2

1. The reason is the highly atypical U.S. tax law, of course, turning the U.S. citizenship into a very costly legal status for the American expats abroad to possess, as we will see in chapter 4.

2. B. Anderson, *Imagined Communities: Reflections on the Origin and Spread of Nationalism* (New York: Verso, 1983).

3. Å. Seierstad, *One of Us: The Story of a Massacre in Norway—and Its Aftermath* (New York: Farrar, Straus and Giroux, 2015).

4. M. Yousafzai and C. Lamb, *I Am Malala* (New York: Little, Brown & Co., 2013).

5. R. Bellamy, *Citizenship* (Oxford: Oxford University Press, 2008).

6. B. Milanovic, "Global Income Inequality by the Numbers," *World Bank Policy Research,* no. 6259 (2012).

7. J. Carens, "Aliens and Citizens" *Review of Politics* 49 (1987): 251–252.

8. B. Milanovic, *Global Inequality* (Cambridge, MA: Belknap Press of Harvard University, 2016), 125.

9. Ibid., 149.

10. J. Tully, *On Global Citizenship* (London: Bloomsbury Academic, 2014), 32.

11. L. Bosniak, *The Citizen and the Alien* (Princeton, NJ: Princeton University Press, 2006), 5–9 and further.

12. T. Agarin, *A Cat's Lick: Democratisation and Minority Communities in the Post-Soviet Baltic* (Amsterdam: Rodopi, 2010).

13. ERR, "Language Inspectorate to Investigate Language Law Violations in Narva City Council," Eesti Rahvusringhääling, November 2, 2015, https://news.err.ee/117099/language-inspectorate-to-investigate-language-law -violations-in-narva-city-council.

14. LSM, "Riga Mayor Will Go to Court over Russian Language Fine," LSM, public broadcasting of Latvia, March 14, 2017, https://eng.lsm.lv/article/society/society/riga-mayor-will-go-to-court-over-russian-language-fine .a227995/.

15. The best contribution on this curious point is R. Rael, *Borderwall as Architecture* (Berkeley: University of California Press, 2016).

16. Carens, "Aliens and Citizens," 251, 270.

17. The diasporas abroad are at least as large as the resident population: J. Resende-Santos, "Cape Verde," *International Migration* 54 (2016): 82, 87–88; International Organization for Migration (IOM), *Migration Data Portal* (2017), https://migrationdataportal.org/data?i=stock_abs_origin&t=2017&cm49 =132.

18. 2016 and 2015 estimates, respectively.

19. R. Brubaker, *Citizenship and Nationhood in France and Germany* (Cambridge, MA: Harvard University Press, 1992), 23.

20. The population of the fifty-one very high HDI countries is 1.3 billion.

21. As presented in Elden's insightful book: S. Elden, *The Birth of Territory* (Chicago: University of Chicago Press, 2013), 22.

22. L. Siedentop, *Inventing the Individual* (Cambridge, MA: Belknap Press of Harvard University, 2014).

23. K. Kim, *Aliens in Mediaeval Law* (Cambridge: Cambridge University Press, 2000) 195; italics in original.

24. S. Navot, *Constitutional Law of Israel* (Dordrecht: Kluwer, 2007), para. 513, discussing the "Citizenship by Virtue of Return."

25. J.-M. Araiza, "Good Neighbourliness as the Limit of Extra-territorial Citizenship: The Case of Hungary and Slovakia," in *Good Neighbourliness in the European Legal Context*, ed. D Kochenov and E. Basheska (Leiden: Brill Nijhoff, 2015), 114.

26. EUDO, "EUDO CITIZENSHIP Database on Modes of Acquisition of Citizenship in Europe," http://eudo-citizenship.eu/admin/?p=dataEUCIT&application=modesAcquisition.

27. K. Surak, "Global Citizenship 2.0—The Growth of Citizenship by Investment Programs," *Investment Migration Council Paper*, no. 3 (2016).

28. A. Twomey, "Section 44 of the Constitution," *Australasian Parliamentary Review* 32 (2018): 6–21. It is interesting to note that the approach to the political rights of dual citizens is directly the opposite in the law of the Council of Europe, binding on forty-seven European states following the European Court of Human Rights decision in *Tănase v. Moldova,* App. No. 7/08, April 27, 2010.

29. R. Hansen, *Citizenship and Immigration in Postwar Britain* (Oxford: Oxford University Press, 2000), 213–221.

30. High Court of Australia, *Re Xenophon* C18/2017 [2017] HCA 45, October 27, 2017, paras. 131 and 135.

31. Art. 96(1)(b) of the Colombian Constitution of 1991 (as amended).

32. S. Morrison, "Foreign in a Domestic Sense: American Samoa and the Last U.S. Nationals," *Hastings Constitutional Law Quarterly* 41 (2013): 71, 84–86. For a historical account of the status of U.S. "non-citizen nationals," see D. O. McGovney, "Our Non-Citizen Nationals, Who Are They?," in *Legal Essays in Tribute to Orrin Kip McMurray*, ed. M. Radin and A. M. Kidd (Berkeley: University of California Press, 1935), 323–374.

33. B. K. Blitz, "Neither Seen nor Heard: Compound Deprivation among Stateless Children," in *Children without a State*, ed. J. Bhabha (Cambridge, MA: MIT Press, 2011), 43–66.

34. Art. 13, Law of the Republic of Belarus of 1 August 2002 No. 136-Z on Citizenship of the Republic of Belarus.

35. A shorthand of *bidūn jinsīyah*—"without nationality": E. A. Chung, "Citizenship in Non-Western Contexts," in *The Oxford Handbook of Citizenship*, ed. A. Shachar, R. Bauböck, I. Bloemraad, and M. Vink (Oxford: Oxford University Press, 2017), 431, 435–436.

36. The deportees are in fact sent to Thailand, as Atossa Abrahamian has demonstrated: A. A. Abrahamian, *The Cosmopolites* (New York: Columbia Global Reports, 2015).

37. Constitutional Court of Latvia, March 7, 2005, Case No. 2004-15-0106, para. 15 (stating that "non-citizens" were a "new, up to that time unknown category of persons" but reiterating they are not "stateless persons").

38. The condemnation of this fact by key international organizations including the UN, OSCE, and the Council of Europe is universal. Cf. I. Brande-Kehre and I. Pūce, "Nationhood and Identity," in *How Democratic Is Latvia: Audit of Democracy*, ed. J. Rozenvalds (Riga: University of Latvia and the University of Latvia Advanced Social and Political Research Institute, 2015), 23–29. The Supreme Court of Latvia even decided to allow the parents to register their child as a "non-citizen" in the cases when one of the parents holds a nationality of a foreign country: Senate of the Supreme Court of Latvia, April 13, 2005, Case No. SKA-136.

39. G.-R. de Groot, "Children, Their Right to a Nationality and Child Statelessness," in *Nationality and Statelessness under International Law*, ed. A. Edwards and L. Van Waas (Cambridge: Cambridge University Press, 2014), 144–168. This is exactly the factual situation that played out in the *Ruiz Zambrano* case in front of the European Court of Justice: a Colombian couple did not register their Belgian-born offspring to ensure that the children would get a much better Belgian citizenship. Case C-34/09 *Ruiz Zambrano* [2011] ECR I-1177.

40. A. H. Midtbøen, S. R. Birkvad, and M. B. Erdal, "Citizenship in the Nordic Countries" (Copenhagen: Nordic Council of Ministers & TemaNord, 2018), 62–63.

41. Soviet citizens who tried to renounce citizenship were treated as mentally ill: *Abuse of Psychiatry in the Soviet Union: Hearing before the Subcommittee on Human Rights and International Organizations of the Committee of Foreign Affairs and the Commission on Security and Cooperation in Europe, House of Representatives, 98th Congress, First Session, September 20, 1983* (Washington, DC: U.S. Government Printing Office, 1983), 76.

42. A. F. Fahrmeir, "Nineteenth-Century German Citizenships," *The Historical Journal* 40 (1997): 721.

43. E. Lohr, *Russian Citizenship: From Empire to Soviet Union* (Cambridge, MA: Harvard University Press, 2012), 177 et seq.

44. C. Schönberger, "European Citizenship as Federal Citizenship," *European Review of Public Law* 19 (2009): 61.

45. The British Nationality Act requires individuals to swear by "Almighty God" while other nations' oaths usually invoke the reigning monarch, the state, the nation, and the constitution.

46. Over the last decade the failure rate has been in the range of 68.8 percent in Denmark, as opposed to 22 percent in the UK, 9 percent in the United States, and 1.1 percent in Germany.

47. Instituto Nacional de Estadistica, "Statistics on Acquisition of Spanish Nationality of Residents," press release, December 5, 2017, 2, https://www.ine.es/en/prensa/aner_2016_en.pdf.

48. A. O. Law, "The Diversity Visa Lottery," *Journal of American Ethnic History* 21 (2002): 3–29.

49. G. Tintori, *Fardelli d'Italia? Conseguenze Nazionali e Transnazionali delle Politiche di Cittadinanza Italiane* (Rome: Carocci, 2009); G. Tintori, "Italy's State-driven Creation of Transnational Emigration Politics," *International Migration 49* (2011): 168, 172–176.

50. S. Navot, *Constitutional Law of Israel* (Dordrecht: Kluwer, 2007). On the tax, see Israel Tax Authority, "Tax Break Package for New Immigrants and Returning Residents," https://taxes.gov.il/english/incometax/documents/taxbreakpackagefornewimmigrantsandreturningresidents.pdf.

51. P. Buwalda, *They Did Not Dwell Alone: Jewish Emigration from the Soviet Union, 1967–1990* (Washington, DC: Woodrow Wilson Center, 1997), 41–46; M. Knisbacher, "*Aliyah* of Soviet Jews," *Harvard International Law Journal* 14 (1973): 89.

52. H. U. Jessurun d'Oliveira, "Iberian Nationality Legislation and Sephardic Jews," *European Constitutional Law Review* 11 (2015): 13.

53. For a very good introduction, see U. Belavusau and A. Gliszczyńska-Grabias, eds., *Law and Memory* (Cambridge: Cambridge University Press, 2017).

54. E. Renan, *Qu'est-ce qu'un nation?* (Paris: Press-Pocket, coll. Agora, [1882] 1992).

55. What constitutes a "right conversion" is a subject of a constant heated debate and was even at issue in front of the UK Supreme Court, among many other courts: *R (E) v. Governing Body of JFS* [2009] *UKSC* 15.

56. F. Duchêne, *Jean Monnet* (New York, London: W. W. Norton & Company, 1994), 54–55.

57. Public Law 107–209, August 6, 2002, 107th Congress Joint Resolution Conferring Honorary Citizenship of the United States Posthumously on Marie Joseph Paul Yves Roche Gilbert du Motier, the Marquis de Lafayette 116 STAT. 931. The honor was granted, inter alia, since "General Lafayette, voluntarily put forth his own money and risked his life for the freedom of Americans."

58. K. Rygiel, "Dying to Live: Migrant Deaths and Citizenship Politics along European Borders," *Citizenship Studies* 20 (2016): 545, 550: "Upon visiting the

island, former Italian Prime Minister, Enrico Letta, announced [that the dead] would be buried in a state funeral. Shipwreck survivors, however, were arrested, detained and threatened with fines as illegal migrants."

59. Research shows that not only the naturalization certificates, but also the birthright citizenship of the impressed sailors was not recognized by the British: D. Brunsman, "Subjects vs. Citizens: Impressment and Identity in the Anglo-American Atlantic," *Journal of the Early Republic* 30 (2010): 557, 573.

60. "Convention between the United States of America and Great Britain, Relative to Naturalization, Concluded May 13, 1870, Ratifications Exchanged August 10, 1870, Proclaimed by the President of the United States, September 16, 1870," Treaties and Conventions between the United States and Other Powers, Since July 4, 1776, rev. ed. (Washington, DC: Government Printing Office, 1873), 405.

61. B. Herzog, *Expatriation in America from the Colonial Era* (New York: NYU Press, 2017), 57.

62. Lohr, *Russian Citizenship*, 109–110.

63. As reported in P. J. Spiro, *At Home in Two Countries* (New York: NYU Press, 2016), 23.

64. J. M. M. Chan, "The Right to a Nationality as a Human Right," *Human Rights Law Journal* 12, no. 1–2 (1991): 1

65. S. Legomsky, "Comment: Dual Nationality and Military Service," in *Rights and Duties of Dual Nationals*, ed. D. A. Martin and K. Hailbronner (Boston: Brill, 2003), 264–268.

66. P. J. Spiro, "Trump's Anti-Muslim Plan Is Awful. And Constitutional," *New York Times*, December 8, 2015, https://www.nytimes.com/2015/12/10/opinion/trumps-anti-muslim-plan-is-awful-and-constitutional.html.

67. C. Gall, "Americans Jailed after Failed Coup in Turkey Are Hostages to Politics," *New York Times*, October 7, 2017, https://www.nytimes.com/2017/10/07/world/europe/turkey-american-detainees.html.

68. D. Stasiulis and D. Ross, "Security, Flexible Sovereignty, and the Perils of Multiple Citizenship," *Citizenship Studies* 10 (2006): 329; C. Forcese, "The Capacity to Protect: Diplomatic Protection of Dual Nationals in the 'War on Terror,'" *European Journal of International Law* 17 (2006): 369.

69. P. J. Spiro, "Dual Citizenship as a Human Right," *International Journal of Constitutional Law* 8 (2010): 111.

70. U.S. Supreme Court, *Afroyim v. Rusk* 387 U.S. 253 (1967).

71. Cf. A. M. Boll, *Multiple Nationality and International Law* (Dordrecht: Martinus Nijhoff, 2007).

72. At the canton level this only happened in 1991, following a court decision: Federal Supreme Court of Switzerland, *Appenzell Innerhoden* case (BGE 116 Ia 359). Cf. L. A. Banaszak, *Why Movements Succeed or Fail—Opportunity, Culture, and the Struggle for Woman Suffrage* (Princeton, NJ: Princeton University Press, 1996), 3–5, 12–19.

73. C. L. Bredbenner, *A Nationality of Her Own* (Berkeley: University of California Press, 1998).

74. For more splendid details, see M. D. Goldhaber, *A People's History of the European Court of Human Rights* (New Brunswick, NJ: Rutgers University Press, 2007), 15–25.

75. European Court of Human Rights, *Marckx v. Belgium* (1979) App. No. 6833/74, June 13, 1979, Series A, no. 31.

76. A. Kollontai, *The Autobiography of a Sexually Emancipated Communist Woman*, trans. S. Attanasio (Freiberg: Herder and Herder, 1971).

77. P. Sherwell, "Price of Loving a Turkmen Girl Is Now USD 50.000," *The Telegraph*, July 22, 2001, https://www.telegraph.co.uk/news/worldnews/asia/turkmenistan/1334919/Price-of-loving-a-Turkmen-girl-is-now-50000.html.

78. Needless to say, Turkmenistan is not the place to look for marriage equality.

79. E.g., B. Kundrus and P. Szobar, "Forbidden Company: Romantic Relationships between Germans and Foreigners, 1939 to 1945," *Journal of the History of Sexuality* 11 (2002): 201.

80. P. Weil, *The Sovereign Citizen* (Philadelphia: University of Pennsylvania Press, 2012), 57 et seq.

81. While the situation of other regions under U.S. control, like Puerto Rico, that are overwhelmingly populated by minorities is similar in terms of political rights, the inhabitants now at least hold U.S. citizenship. N. De Genova and A. Y. Ramos-Zayas, *Latino Crossings: Mexicans, Puerto Ricans, and the Politics of Race and Citizenship* (London: Routledge, 2004).

82. P. Christiaans and M. Schrover, "Het Oudpaspoortarchief (1950–1959)," in *Bronnen betreffende de registraties van vreemdelingen in Nederland in de negentiende en twntigste eeuw*, ed. M Schrover (The Hague: Instituut voor Nederlandse Geschiedenis 2002), 156.

83. The sexism of the racial miscegenation laws was of course universal and was not confined to the Dutch Empire. In all the overtly racist U.S. states, prior to the civil rights movement, white women were consistently punished more harshly than white males for any relationship with an African American. Not only was marriage prohibited, but "sharing a room at night" and "traveling

together" were as well. The U.S. Supreme Court only found such statutes unconstitutional in the 1960s: *McLaughlin v. Florida*, 379 U.S. 184 (1964), 188; *Loving v. Virginia*, 388 U.S. 1 (1967). Cf. W. Sollors, ed., *Interracialism* (Oxford: Oxford University Press, 2000).

84. M. Saada, *Empire's Children* (Chicago: University of Chicago Press, 2012).

85. B. H. Isaac, *The Invention of Racism in Classical Antiquity* (Princeton, NJ: Princeton University Press, 2004).

86. The data amassed under the auspices of the Quality of Nationality Index proves this point overwhelmingly: even setting aside human development and economic opportunities, the nationalities of the African continent are the worst-performing in the world in terms of freedom of visa-free travel and settlement abroad for work.

87. P. Bologov, "Will Russia Introduce Visas for Central Asia?," Intersection Project, June 6, 2016, http://intersectionproject.eu/article/russia-world/will -russia-introduce-visas-central-asia.

88. At the political level this could be illustrated by "The Economist Intelligence Unit's Democracy Index" (updated annually), *The Economist*, https:// www.eiu.com/topic/democracy-index. All of the non-Western former colonies are at the bottom of the index, thus entirely failing in self-governance (as discussed in chapter 5). At the level of economic development and wealth accumulation, these countries are structurally behind the rest of the globe, necessarily overwhelmingly undermining the chances of own citizens to achieve economic success as Milanovic has shown. At the level of freedom of travel and settlement around the world, the majority of the former colonies outside the West grant citizenships at the very bottom of world rankings, as demonstrated by the Quality of Nationality Index, op. cit.

89. Milanovic, *Global Inequality*, 173.

90. Bredbenner, *A Nationality of Her Own*.

91. S. Munshi, "Immigration, Imperialism, and the Legacies of Indian Exclusion," *Yale Journal of Law and Humanities* 28 (2016): 51.

92. D. L. DeLaet, *U.S. Immigration Policy in an Age of Rights* (Westport, CT: Greenwood, 2000).

93. See South Africa, Bantu Homelands Citizenship Act, 1970.

94. S. Ally and A. Lissoni, eds., *New Histories of South Africa's Apartheid-Era Bantustans* (London: Routledge, 2017). See also, on the operation of the law, J. Dugard, "South Africa's Independent Homelands," *Denver Journal of International Law and Policy* 10 (1980): 11.

95. B. Attwood, *The 1967 Referendum: Race, Power and the Australian Constitution* (Acton, ACT, Australia: Aboriginal Studies Press, 2007).

96. J. E. Okolo, "Free Movement of Persons in ECOWAS and Nigeria's Expulsion of Illegal Aliens," *World Today* 40 (1984): 428.

97. UAE Federal Law No. 17 of 1972 Concerning Nationality and Passports with its amendments: Art. 8 sets the naturalization time requirement for non-Arabs at twenty years of residence; Arabs naturalize after seven years (Art. 6); Omanis, Qataris, and Bahrainis after three years (Art. 5).

98. For a general overview of racist elements in the contemporary citizenship regulation in Africa, see, e.g., B. Manby, *Citizenship Law in Africa* (New York, NY: Open Society Foundations, 2010).

99. U.S. Supreme Court, *United States v. Bhagat Singh Thind* 261 U.S. 204 (1923). Such a "scientific" approach to classifying Americans by race resulted in a remarkably self-contradictory jurisprudence.

100. I. Hany-Lopez, *White by Law: The Legal Construction of Race* (New York: NYU Press, 1996).

101. Munshi, "Immigration, Imperialism, and the Legacies of Indian Exclusion."

102. Y. Harpaz, *Citizenship 2.0: Dual Nationality as a Global Asset* (Princeton, NJ: Princeton University Press, 2019).

103. L. Chamberlain, *Lenin's Private War: The Voyage of the Philosophy Steamer and the Exile of the Intelligentsia* (New York: St. Martin's Press, 2007).

104. G. Ginsburgs, "The Soviet Union and the Problem of Refugees and Displaced Persons 1917–1956," *American Journal of International Law* 51 (1957): 325.

105. J. Q. Whitman, *Hitler's American Model* (Princeton, NJ: Princeton University Press, 2017).

106. J. Kim, *Contested Embrace: Transborder Membership Politics in Twentieth-Century Korea* (Stanford, CA: Stanford University Press, 2016).

107. P. M. Polian, *Against Their Will: The History and Geography of Forced Migrations in the USSR* (Budapest: CEU Press, 2004).

108. I. Müller, *Hitler's Justice* (Cambridge, MA: Harvard University Press, 1991).

109. H. U. Jessurun d'Oliveira, ed., *Ontjoodst door de wetenschap. De wetenschappelijke en menselijke integriteit van Arie de Froe onder de bezetting* (Amsterdam: Amsterdam University Press, 2015).

110. S. D. Rutland, "A Reassessment of the Dutch Record during the Holocaust," in *Remembering for the Future the Holocaust in an Age of Genocide*, ed. J. K. Roth, E. Maxwell, M. Levy, and W. Whitworth (Basingstoke: Palgrave Macmillan, 2001), 527.

111. B. Frommer, *National Cleansing: Retribution against Nazi Collaborators in Postwar Czechoslovakia* (Cambridge: Cambridge University Press, 2005).

112. M. Myant, "New Research on February 1948 in Czechoslovakia," in *1948 and 1968—Dramatic Milestones in Czech and Slovak History*, ed. L. Cashman (London: Routledge, 2009), 57.

113. Kim, *Contested Embrace*.

114. Not returning from abroad was considered treason in Soviet Law (e.g., Art. 64(a) of the RSFSR Penal Code of 1960) and was only found unconstitutional in 1995: Constitutional Court of the Russian Federation, Decision 17-P, 20 Dec. 1995.

115. The history of decolonization is also a history of deep ethnic discrimination: the majority of the citizens of European and Indian origin left the former African colonies; Russians from the former Soviet Republics in Central Asia fled to the former imperial center; Jewish communities all around the Middle East have been decimated—these histories are as countless as they are well known.

116. R. Evans, "The Perils of Being a Borderland People: On the Lhotshampas of Bhutan," *Contemporary South Asia* 18 (2010): 25.

117. N. Cheesman, "How in Myanmar 'National Races' Came to Surpass Citizenship and Exclude Rohingya," *Journal of Contemporary Asia* 47 (2017): 461.

118. D. Howard, "Development, Racism, and Discrimination in the Dominican Republic," *Development in Practice* 17 (2007): 725.

119. R. Mohan, "A Crackdown on Minorities in Northeast India Threatens to Strip 4 Million People of Citizenship," *TIME*, August 14, 2018, http://time.com/5366462/india-assam-citizenship/.

120. T. Bloom, K. Tonkiss, and P. Cole, "Providing a Framework for Understanding Statelessness," in *Understanding Statelessness*, ed. T. Bloom, K. Tonkiss, and P. Cole (London: Routledge, 2017), 4.

121. I. Štiks, *Nations and Citizens in Yugoslavia and Post-Yugoslav States* (London: Bloomsbury Academic, 2015).

122. Nationality, Immigration and Asylum Act 2002 s. 40(2).

123. P. Spiro, "Expatriating Terrorists," *Fordham Law Review* 82 (2014): 2169.

124. The White House Office of the Press Secretary, "Fact Sheet: U.S. Policy Standards and Procedures for the Use of Force in Counterterrorism Operations Outside the United States and Areas of Active Hostilities," Obama White House Archives, May 23, 2013, https://obamawhitehouse.archives.gov/the-press-office/2013/05/23/fact-sheet-us-policy-standards-and-procedures-use-force-counterterrorism.

125. Araiza, "Good Neighbourliness as the Limit of Extra-territorial Citizenship."

126. R. Mandel, *Cosmopolitan Anxieties: Turkish Challenges to Citizenship and Belonging in Germany* (Durham, NC: Duke University, 2008).

127. G. Visokam, *Acting Like a State: Kosovo and the Everyday Making of Statehood* (London: Routledge, 2018).

128. R. H. Keyserlink, *Austria in World War II* (Kingston: McGill-Queen's University Press, 1988), 22.

129. Cudenhove-Kalergi founded the Pan-European movement right after World War I: the first high-level continental political move for European unification: R. N. von Coudenhove-Kalergi, *History of the Paneuropean Movement, from 1922–1962* (Paneuropean Union, 1962).

130. Atossa Araxia Abrahamian was right to note, in the pages of the *New York Review*, that the movie is, essentially, about getting the right papers in turbulent times: "The New Passport Poor," May 21, 2018, https://www.nybooks .com/daily/2018/05/21/the-new-passport-poor/.

131. Max Planck Encyclopaedia of Public International Law, vol. 8, *Human Rights and the Individual in Public International Law—International Economic Relations*, "Nationality" (Amsterdam: North Holland, 1985).

132. The EU, to give one example, is meticulous in applying this age-old rule: European Union External Action, "The EU Non-recognition Policy for Crimea and Sevastopol: Fact Sheet" (Bruxelles, December 12, 2017), https:// eeas.europa.eu/headquarters/headquarters-Homepage/37464/eu-non-recog nition-policy-crimea-and-sevastopol-fact-sheet_en.

133. International Court of Justice, *Nottebohm Case* (*Liechtenstein v. Guatemala*) 1955 ICJ 4.

134. Paying your way into the legal status in a state in the German empire was a necessary step for changing both residence and citizenship within the empire, which remained in force in Liechtenstein at the time: A. F. Fahrmeir, "Nineteenth-Century German Citizenships: A Reconsideration," *The Historical Journal* 40 (1997): 721. On the current state of investment migration, see C. Kälin, Ius Doni *in International Law and EU Law* (Boston: Brill, 2019).

135. The most frequent mistake is to present the *Nottebohm* case as a choice of law rule in the cases of multiple nationality, which it is obviously not, since Nottebohm had one nationality only and was deprived of any due process of law regardless.

136. See, in particular, International Court of Justice, *Nottebohm Case*, dissenting opinion of Judge Klæstad [1955] ICJ Rep 4, 28.

137. A. Sironi, "Nationality of Individuals in Public International Law: A Functional Approach," in *The Changing Role of Nationality in International Law*, ed. A. Annoni and S. Forlati (London: Routledge, 2014), 54–68.

138. European Court of Justice, Case C-369/90 *Micheletti* [1992] ECR I-4239.

139. Ibid.

140. Opinion of Advocate General Tesauro in Case C-369/90 *Micheletti* [1992] ECR I-4239, para. 5.

141. E.g., D. Goldhagen, *Hitler's Willing Executioners* (New York: Knopf, 1996).

142. International Court of Justice, *Nottebohm Case* (*Liechtenstein v. Guatemala*) 1955 ICJ 4, 20.

143. Brubaker, *Citizenship and Nationhood in France and Germany*, 23.

Chapter 3

1. T. H. Marshall, *Class, Citizenship, and Social Development* (Chicago: University of Chicago Press, 1977).

2. H. Maine, *Ancient Law: Its Connection with the Early History of Society, and Its Relation to Modern Ideas* (London: J. M. Dent & Sons Ltd., [1861] 1917). Cf. K. I. Schmidt, "Henry Maine's 'Modern Law': From Status to Contract and Back Again?," *American Journal of Comparative Law* 65 (2017): 145.

3. J. Mueller, "Democracy and Ralph's Pretty Good Grocery: Elections, Equality, and the Minimal Human Being," *American Journal of Political Science* 36 (1992): 983, 988.

4. Marshall, *Class, Citizenship, and Social Development*.

5. L. Ferrajoli, "Dai diritti del cittadino ai diritti della persona," in *La cittadinanza: Appartenenza, identità, diritti*, ed. D. Zolo (Rome/Bari: Laterza, 1994), 264–265.

6. Note that neither Spanish nor English are among the official languages on the island of Curaçao, although both are very widely spoken. The languages in law and the languages spoken in fact sometimes fail to overlap almost entirely and this is one such example: the nonofficial spoken languages entered into official use (passport stamps).

7. See the court decision recognizing far-reaching effects of the 1956 Dutch-American Friendship Treaty for the Dutch overseas: Joint Court of Justice of Aruba, Curaçao, Sint Maarten, and of Bonaire, Sint Eustatius, and Saba, Case HLAR 69566/14, ECLI:NL:OGHACMB:2014:92.

8. J. Torpey, *The Invention of the Passport* (Cambridge: Cambridge University Press, 2000), 19.

9. F. J. Conte, "Sink or Swim Together: Citizenship, Sovereignty, and Free Movement in the European Union and the United States," *University of Miami Law Review* 31 (2007): 331, 365–375.

10. U.S. Supreme Court, *Edwards v. California*, 314 U.S. 160 (1941).

11. C. O'Brien, *Unity in Adversity: EU Citizenship, Social Justice and the Cautionary Tale of the UK* (Oxford: Hart Publishing, 2017).

12. N. Werth, "The Russian Card," in C. Watner and W. McElroy, eds., *National Identification Systems* (Jefferson, NC: McFarland, 2003), 116–119.

13. K. W. Chan, "Internal Migration in China," in H. Mallee and F. N. Pieke, eds., *Internal and International Migration* (Abingdon: Routledge, 2014), 49; E. Lohr, *Russian Citizenship: From Empire to Soviet Union* (Cambridge, MA: Harvard University Press, 2012).

14. I. Zhelvakova, *Herzen* (Moscow: Molodaja Gvardija, ZhZL, 2010).

15. L. Cecil, *Wilhelm II: Volume 2* (Chapel Hill, NC: University of North Carolina Press, 2000), 212 and 321.

16. C. Dunn, *Brutality Garden: Tropicália and the Emergence of a Brazilian Counter-culture* (Chapel Hill: University of North Carolina Press, 2001).

17. E. Tamkin, "The Man without a State," *Foreign Policy*, August 22, 2017, https://foreignpolicy.com/2017/08/22/the-man-without-a-state-misha-saakashvili-georgia-ukraine/.

18. On Trotsky's life, see, e.g., Isaac Deutscher's majestic three-volume *Prophet* series, published by Oxford (Oxford: Oxford University Press, 1954, 1959, 1963).

19. H. Arendt, *The Origins of Totalitarianism* (New York: Harcourt Brace & Co., 1979 [1951]), 226.

20. R. Plender, *International Migration Law* (Dordrecht: Martinus Nijhoff, 1988), 133.

21. N. M. Rajkovic, *The Politics of International Law and Compliance: Serbia, Croatia and the Hague Tribunal* (Abingdon: Routledge, 2011).

22. G. Partos, "No Extradition for Croatian Generals," *BBC News*, October 18, 1999, http://news.bbc.co.uk/2/hi/europe/478647.stm.

23. B. Anderson, M. J. Gibney, and E. Paoletti, "Citizenship, Deportation and the Boundaries of Belonging," *Citizenship Studies* 51 (2011): 547. Curiously, the European Union, one of the most rights-aware jurisdictions in the world, has abolished this right in the interactions between EU member states: the European Arrest Warrant makes the surrender of a state's own citizens obligatory and operates all over the territory of the European Union. Cf. R. Colson, "Domesticating the European Arrest Warrant: European Criminal Law between Fragmentation and Acculturation," in *EU Criminal Justice and the Challenges of Diversity*, ed. R.Colson (Cambridge: Cambridge University Press, 2016).

24. P. Karp, "Australian Government to Replace 457 Temporary Work Visa," *The Guardian*, April 18 2017, https://www.theguardian.com/australia-news/2017/apr/18/australian-government-abolish-457-temporary-work-visa.

25. European Court of Human Rights, *Beldjoudi v. France*, App. No. 12083/86, judgment of March 26, 1992. Y. Ronen, "The Ties That Bind: Family and Private Life as Bars to the Deportation of Immigrants," *International Journal of Law in Context* 8 (2012): 283.

26. European Court of Human Rights, *Beldjoudi v. France*, App. No. 12083/86, judgment of March 26 1992, Judge Martens, concurring, para. 2(2).

27. UN Human Rights Committee, *Stewart v. Canada* U.N. Doc. CCPR/C/58D/538/1993 (1996).

28. European Court of Human Rights, *Jeunesse v. Netherlands,* App. No. 12738/10, judgment of October 3, 2014.

29. Some academic literature takes on this question without much irony: no matter where one's life is lived the law is the law, so if it says you are illegal for any reason at all, you should be deported, rather than allowed to stay: D. Thym, "Respect for Private and Family Life under Article 8 ECHR in Immigration Cases," *International and Comparative Law Quarterly* 57 (2008) 87.

30. Z. Babar, "Free Movement of People within the Gulf," in *Migration, Free Movement and Regional Integration*, ed. S. Nita, A. Pécoud, P. De Lombaerde, P. de Guchteneire, K. Neyts, and J. Gartland (Paris: UNESCO 2017); 149–170.

31. C. Schenk, "Labor Migration in the Eurasian Union," PONARS Eurasia Policy Memo No. 378 (August 2015), http://www.ponarseurasia.org/sites/default/files/policy-memos-pdf/Pepm378_Schenk_Aug2015.pdf; M. V. Lushnikova, K. S. Ramankulov, and K. L. Tomaszewski, eds., *Jevrazijskoje Trudovoje Pravo* (Moscow: Prospekt, 2017).

32. J. Ukaigwe, *ECOWAS Law* (Cham: Springer, 2016), 186–187.

33. Art. 12, Protocol of OECS Economic Union to the Revised Treaty of Basseterre Establishing the Organization of Eastern Caribbean States Economic Union [2010].

34. D. Acosta Arcarazo, *The National versus the Foreigner in South America: 200 Years of Migration and Citizenship Law* (Cambridge: Cambridge University Press, 2018).

35. R. A. Underwood, "The Amended US Compacts of Free Association with the Federated States of Micronesia and the Republic of the Marshall Islands," *East-West Center Working Paper Pacific Islands Development Series No. 16* (2003): 8, https://scholarspace.manoa.hawaii.edu/handle/10125/3612; D. R. Shuster, "The Republic of Palau and Its Compact, 1995–2009," *Journal of Pacific History* 44 (2009): 325, 327.

36. L. Dyer, "Anglo-Saxon Citizenship," *The Barrister* 3 (1897): 107. The racist and sexist essentials of citizenship were presumed to stay, of course: only the "Anglo-Saxons" were to benefit from the proposal.

37. Acosta Arcarazo, *The National versus the Foreigner in South America: 200 Years of Migration and Citizenship Law.*

38. B. Manby, *Citizenship Law in Africa* (New York: Open Society Foundations, 2010).

39. Anthony, Lord Lester of Herne Hill, "Thirty Years On: The East African Case Revisited," *Public Law* (2002): 52.

40. Ibid.

41. I. Tyler, "Designed to Fail: A Biopolitics of British Citizenship," *Citizenship Studies* 14 (2010): 61.

42. Ethnicity has always been the key driver behind the contents of colonial citizenships: K. Sadiq, "Postcolonial Citizenship," in *The Oxford Handbook of Citizenship*, ed. A. Shachar, R. Bauböck, I. Bloemraad, and M. Vink (Oxford: Oxford University Press, 2017), 178, 180–183.

43. C(68)29, CAB 129/136.

44. European Commission for Human Rights, *East African Asians v. UK*, App. Nos. 4403/70 et al., December 14, 1973.

45. D. Vine, *Island of Shame: The Secret History of the U.S. Military Base on Diego Garcia* (Princeton, NJ: Princeton University Press, 2011).

46. UK House of Lords, *R (On the Application of Bancoult) v. Secretary of State for Foreign and Commonwealth Affairs* [2008] UKHL 61, para. 45.

47. British Indian Ocean Territory (Constitution) Order 2004, para. 9(1): " … no person has the right of abode in the Territory."

48. R. Kassem, "Passport Revocation as Proxy Denaturalization: Examining the Yemen Cases," *Fordham Law Review* 82 (2014): 2099.

49. Tyler, "Designed to Fail."

50. As these rights are subject to a separate authorization granted by the governments of the British Overseas Territories and entered into the respective passports: Ian Hendry and Susan Dickson, eds., *British Overseas Territories Law*, 2nd ed. (Oxford: Hart Publishing, 2018).

51. N. Caspersen, *Unrecognized States* (Oxford: Wiley, 2013).

52. A. Edwards and L. van Waas, eds., *Nationality and Statelessness under International Law* (Cambridge: Cambridge University Press, 2014); P. Weis, *Nationality and Statelessness in International Law*, 2nd ed. (Amsterdam: Sijthoff & Noordhoff, 1979).

53. G. Brock and M. Blake, *Debating Brain Drain* (Oxford: Oxford University Press, 2014).

54. L. Bosniak, "Persons and Citizens in Constitutional Thought," *International Journal of Constitutional Law* 8 (2010): 9.

55. Y. N. Soysal, *Limits of Citizenship* (Chicago: University of Chicago Press, 1994).

56. Ferrajoli, "Dai diritti del cittadino ai diritti della persona," 264.

57. S. Rials, *La Déclaration des droits de l'homme et du citoyen* (Paris: Hachette, 1988).

58. Art. 7 of the Napoleonic Code; Ferrajoli, "Dai diritti del Cittadino ai diritti della persona," 264, 266.

59. C. Joppke, *Citizenship and Immigration* (Cambridge: Polity, 2010).

60. Ferrajoli, "Dai diritti del cittadino ai diritti della persona," 264–265.

61. C. Joppke, "Citizenship in Immigrant States," in *The Oxford Handbook of Citizenship*, ed. A. Shachar, R. Bauböck, I. Bloemraad, and M. Vink (Oxford: Oxford University Press, 2017).

62. J. Carens, *The Ethics of Immigration* (Oxford: Oxford University Press, 2013).

63. M. Cohen-Eliya and I. Porat, *Proportionality and Constitutional Culture* (Cambridge: Cambridge University Press, 2013), 111–113 et seq.

64. A. Magen, "The Democratic Entitlement in an Era of Democratic Recession," *Cambridge Journal of International and Comparative Law* 4 (2015): 1.

Chapter 4

1. G. Williams, "The Concept of Legal Liberty," *Columbia Law Review 56* (1956): 1729.

2. P. Marshall and N. Shea, *Silenced: How Apostasy and Blasphemy Codes Are Choking Freedom Worldwide* (Oxford: Oxford University Press, 2011), esp. 21–34.

3. World Bank Regional Vice-Presidency for Africa, *The Pirates of Somalia* (Washington, DC: World Bank, 2013), xxiv–xxv.

4. T. H. Marshall, *Class, Citizenship, and Social Development* (Chicago: University of Chicago Press, 1977), 9.

5. D. Kochenov, "EU Citizenship without Duties," *European Law Journal 20* (2014): 482.

6. Quite conveniently, under Belgian law you are disqualified from voting for ten years for failing to turn out and vote for fifteen consecutive years.

7. "Wiesenthal Center Protests March of Latvia SS Veterans," Simon Wiesenthal Center, March 15, 2016, http://www.wiesenthal.com/site/apps/nlnet/content.aspx?c=lsKWLbPJLnF&b=8776547&ct=14546335&notoc=1.

8. See Kochenov, "EU Citizenship without Duties," discussing all the key ways to justify the duties paradigm of citizenship.

9. See ibid.

10. Report of the Monitoring Group on Somalia and Eritrea pursuant to Security Council resolution 2182 (2014): Eritrea (July 18, 2011) U.N. Doc. S/2011/433.

11. H. Smith, *North Korea* (Cambridge: Cambridge University Press, 2015), 226.

12. J. C. Hall, "The Worldwide Decline in Conscription," Library of Economics and Liberty, 2011, https://www.econlib.org/library/Columns/y2011/Hallcon scription.html#note_1.

13. As quoted in K. Kim, *Aliens in Mediaeval Law* (Cambridge: Cambridge University Press, 2000), 203.

14. L. Siedentop, *Inventing the Individual* (Cambridge, MA: Harvard University Press, 2014).

15. C. Tilly, *Coercion, Capital, and European States, AD 990–1992* (Cambridge, MA: Blackwell, 1990).

16. M. Walzer, "Civility and Civic Virtue in Contemporary America," *Social Research* 41 (1974): 593.

17. US Supreme Court, *Texas v. Johnson*, 491 U.S. 397 (1989).

18. On the situation in Iraq, see Z. Al-Ali, *The Struggle for Iraq's Future* (New Haven, CT: Yale University Press, 2014).

19. E. Schrecker, *Many Are the Crimes: McCarthyism in America* (Princeton, NJ: Princeton University Press, 1999).

20. A. Pais, *Subtle Is the Lord: The Science and the Life of Albert Einstein* (Oxford: Oxford University Press, 1982), 41, 45.

21. S. Collier, *Carlos Gardel* (Buenos Aires: Editorial Sudamericana, 1988).

22. 8 U.S.C. 1182(a)(10)(E).

23. Reproduced by A. Kuzmin, "Latvian Court Rules against a Protester Who Turned Out against the Annual Waffen SS March," *Defending History*, October 16, 2017, http://defendinghistory.com/latvian-court-rules-that-depicting-nazi -violence-of-1941-on-a-placard-is-illegal/90473.

24. See for the full transcript: F. Vigdorova, "The Trial of Joseph Brodsky," *New England Review* 34 (2014): 183.

25. The constant presumption is that citizens "do not understand" their rights: e.g., point 19, European Parliament, "Resolution of 12 December 2017 on the EU Citizenship Report 2017: Strengthening Citizens' Rights in a Union of Democratic Change" (2017/2069(INI)): "organise an EU-wide information

and *awareness-raising campaign on EU citizenship rights in order to help citizens better understand their rights*" (emphasis added).

26. S. Da Lomba, "Legal Status and Refugee Integration: a UK Perspective," *Journal of Refugee Studies* 23 (2010): 415.

27. L Turcescu and L. Stan, "Religion, Politics and Sexuality in Romania," *Europe-Asia Studies* 57 (2005): 291.

28. Section 40, British Nationality Act, 1981; emphasis added.

29. P. Szobar, "Telling Sexual Stories in the Nazi Courts of Law," *Journal of the History of Sexuality* 11 (2002): 131.

30. J. Q. Whitman, "On Nazi 'Honour' and the New European 'Dignity,'" in *Darker Legacies of Law in Europe*, ed. C. Joerges and N. Singh Ghaleigh (Oxford: Hart Publishing, 2003), 243.

31. Szobar, "Telling Sexual Stories in the Nazi Courts of Law," 131, 146.

32. P. Bourdieu, "The Force of Law," *Hastings Law Journal* 38 (1987): 835, 838.

33. PornHub Insights reported, "In 2017, a large number of Southern states showed their lover [sic.] for interracial porn with 'black girl white guy' being searched there far more often than elsewhere in the United States": "2017 State of the Union," *PornHub*, January 16, 2018, https://www.pornhub.com/insights/2017-state-of-the-union.

34. U.S. Supreme Court, *Dred Scott* 60 U.S. 393 (1857), 420–421.

35. U.S. Supreme Court, *Korematsu v. United States* 323 U.S. 214 (1944). For a detailed discussion, see W. L. Ng, *Japanese American Internment during World War II* (Westport, CT: Greenwood Press, 2002).

36. C. Joppke, *Citizenship and Immigration* (Cambridge; Polity, 2010).

37. US Supreme Court, *Dred Scott* 60 U.S. 393 (1857), 420–421.

38. J. R. Abrams, "Examining Entrenched Masculinities in the Republican Government Tradition," *Virginia Law Review* 114 (2011): 165.

39. M. Howard, *The Invention of Peace* (New Haven, CT: Yale University Press, 2001).

40. Tilly, *Coercion, Capital, and European States*, 28.

41. Howard, *The Invention of Peace*.

42. D. L. Cagliotti, "Dealing with the Enemy Aliens in WWI," *Italian Journal of Public Law* 3 (2012): 180.

43. "Soldiers are killers" was the centerpiece of a key German free speech case and the German Federal Constitutional Court protected it: J. Collings, *Democracy's Guardians: A History of the German Federal Constitutional Court, 1951–2001* (Oxford: Oxford University Press, 2015), 267.

44. K. W. Grundy, *The Militarization of South African Politics* (London: IB Tauris, 1986), 22.

45. E.g., R. Neumann, *Zaharoff: The Armaments King*, trans. R. T. Clarke (London: Allen & Unwin, 1938).

46. M. Walzer, "Civility and Civic Virtue in Contemporary America," *Social Research 41* (1974): 593, 606.

47. Joppke, *Citizenship and Immigration,* 116.

48. E. Weber, *Peasants into Frenchmen* (Stanford, CA: Stanford University Press, 1976).

49. W. Kymlicka, *Multicultural Citizenship* (Oxford: Oxford University Press, 1996).

50. C. Hawley, "A German State Quizzes Muslim Immigrants on Jews, Gays and Swim Lessons," *Spiegel*, January 31, 2006, http://www.spiegel.de/international/muslim-profiling-a-german-state-quizes-muslim-immigrants-on-jews-gays-and-swim-lessons-a-397482.html.

Chapter 5

1. J. Mueller, *Capitalism, Democracy and Ralph's Pretty Good Grocery* (Princeton, NJ: Princeton University Press, 1999).

2. The majority of such interventions are not at all illegal, just as the Irish referendum to amend the Constitution to outlaw abortions won, famously, with the support of American money and extremely conservative groups. The harmful outcome of that political decision took more than quarter of a century to undo, requiring a new referendum (under much stricter rules for foreign funding of campaigns) that reversed the amendment purchased with American money by a 66.4 percent majority in May 2018. M. D. Goldhaber, *A People's History of the European Court of Human Rights* (New Brunswick, NJ: Rutgers University Press, 2007), 26–32.

3. Milanovic is right in noting, "To believe that the rich do not use their money to buy influence and promote policies they like is not simply to be naïve. Such a stance contradicts the key principles of economics as well as the ways in which the rich people have amassed their wealth": B. Milanovic, *Global Inequality* (Cambridge, MA: Belknap Press of Harvard University, 2016), 189.

4. S. D. Schmid, J. T. Arrighi, and R. Bauböck, "ELECLAW Indicators," *RSCAS Explanatory Paper Version 4.0* (2017), http://globalcit.eu/wp-content/uploads/2017/12/ELECLAW_explanatory_paper_version-4.0-_-Jun2017.pdf.

5. J. Q. Whitman, "On Nazi 'Honour' and the New European 'Dignity,'" in *Darker Legacies of Law in Europe*, ed. C. Joerges and N. Singh Ghaleigh (Oxford: Hart Publishing, 2003), 243.

6. Z. Oklopcic, *Beyond the People* (Oxford: Oxford University Press, 2018).

7. K. Meta and A. Nachemson, "Document Purge Targeting Ethnic Vietnamese to Continue," *Phnom Penh Post*, November 29, 2017, https://www.phnompenh post.com/national/document-purge-targeting-ethnic-vietnamese-continue.

8. M. W. Brown, "The Effect of Free Trade, Privatisation and Democracy of the Human Rights Conditions for Minorities in Eastern Europe," *Buffalo Human Rights Law Review* 4 (1998): 275.

9. J. Tully, *Strange Multiplicity: Constitutionalism in an Age of Diversity* (Cambridge: Cambridge University Press, 2012).

10. M. Walzer, *Spheres of Justice* (New York: Basic Books, 1983).

11. R. Mandel, *Cosmopolitan Anxieties: Turkish Challenges to Citizenship and Belonging in Germany* (Durham, NC: Duke University Press, 2008).

12. R. Dahl, *After the Revolution?* (New Haven, CT: Yale University Press, 1970), 64–67.

13. R. C. Visek, "Creating Ethnic Electorate through Legal Restorationism: Citizenship Rights in Estonia," *Harvard International Law Journal* 38 (1997): 315.

14. S. Morrison, "Foreign in a Domestic Sense: American Samoa and the Last U.S. Nationals," *Hastings Constitutional Law Quarterly* 41 (2013): 71.

15. J.-M. Araiza and O. Vonk, "Report on Citizenship Law: Myanmar," RSCAS/ GLOBALCIT-CR 2017/14.

16. T. Agarin, *A Cat's Lick: Democratisation and Minority Communities in the Post-Soviet Baltic* (Amsterdam: Rodopi, 2010).

17. H. Lardy, "Citizenship and the Right to Vote," *Oxford Journal of Legal Studies* 17 (1997): 75.

18. European Commission for Human Rights, *X v. UK*, App. No. 7730/76, Commission decision of February 28, 1979.

19. J. Shaw, *The Transformation of Citizenship in the European Union* (Cambridge: Cambridge University Press, 2007).

20. J. B. Raskin, "Legal Aliens, Local Citizens," *University of Pennsylvania Law Review* 141 (1993): 1391.

21. R. Bauböck, "Stakeholder Citizenship and Transnational Political Participation," *Fordham Law Review* 75 (2007): 2393, 2397. On "stakeholder citizenship," see P. Spiro, "Stakeholder Citizenship Will Not Save Citizenship," in R. Bauböck, *Democratic Inclusion: Rainer Bauböck in Dialogue* (Manchester: Manchester University Press, 2017).

22. ACE Electoral Knowledge Network, "Out of Country Voting," https:// aceproject.org/ace-en/topics/va/onePage; International Institute for Democracy and Electoral Assistance, 2007.

23. *The Economist*, "The Economist Intelligence Unit's Democracy Index" (updated annually), https://www.eiu.com/topic/democracy-index.

24. Higher than the number needed to swing the vote—"Vote Leave" won by 1,269,501 votes.

25. K. Armstrong, *Brexit Time* (Cambridge: Cambridge University Press, 2018).

26. T. Gumrukcu and T. Escritt, "Netherlands Bars Turkish Ministers as Rally Dispute Escalates," *Reuters*, March 11, 2017, https://www.reuters.com/article/us-turkey-europe-netherlands/netherlands-bars-turkish-ministers-as-rally-dispute-escalates-idUSKBN16I07O.

27. European Court of Justice, Case C-300/04, *Eman and Sevinger* [2006] ECR I-8055, para. 59.

28. European Court of Human Rights, *Sevinger and Eman v. the Netherlands*, App. Nos. 17173/07 and 17180/07, Third Section, September 6, 2007.

29. All those who naturalize in the Caribbean colonies pass two language tests: the language of the respective island plus Dutch, compared with only Dutch in Europe. The law installing discrimination has been passed in The Hague of course, where the Caribbean Dutch citizens are not represented: G.-R. de Groot and E. Mijts, "De onwenselijkheid van een dubbele taaltoets voor naturalisandi in Aruba en de Nederlandse Antillen" *Migrantenrecht* 24 (2009): 366.

30. This is one of the explanations behind the steep growth of the citizenship by investment industry over the last decades: Kälin, Ius Doni *in International Law and EU Law*.

31. Y. Harpaz, *Citizenship 2.0: Dual Nationality as a Global Asset* (Princeton, NJ: Princeton University Press, 2019).

32. Unlike the people, money always had options to flow across borders easily: V. Ogle, "Archipelago Capitalism: Tax Havens, Offshore Money, and the State, 1950–1970" *American Historical Review* 122 (2017): 1431.

33. Parliamentary Assembly of the Council of Europe Report (Rapporteurs Aguilar and Guirado), *Links between Europeans Living Abroad and Their Countries of Origin* (1999), PACE Doc. 8339.

34. D. Aliano, "Citizenship and Belonging: The Case of the Italian Vote Abroad" *Ethnic Studies Review* 33 (2010): 36.

35. S. Pogonyi, *Extra-Territorial Ethnic Politics, Discourses and Identities in Hungary* (Basingstoke: Palgrave Macmillan, 2017), 167.

36. Foreign Account Tax Compliance Act, Pub. L. No. 111–147, 124 Stat. 71 (2010), 97–117.

37. P. J. Spiro, "Citizenship Overreach," *Michigan Journal of International Law* 38 (2017): 167.

38. Fewer people have renounced their citizenship under Trump than under Obama: A. Mitchel, "Number of Americans Renouncing Their U.S. Citizenship Fell in 2017, The First Decline in Five Years," *International Tax Blog*, February 8, 2018, http://intltax.typepad.com/intltax_blog/2018/02/2017-fourth-quarter-published-expatriates-first-annual-decrease-in-five-years.html.

39. D. Kostakopoulou, "Why Naturalization?," *Perspectives on European Politics and Society* 4 (2003): 85.

40. C. Joppke, *Citizenship and Immigration* (Cambridge: Polity, 2010), 54.

41. E.g., A. Shachar, "Dangerous Liaisons: Money and Citizenship,'" in *Debating Transformations of National Citizenships*, ed. R. Bauböck (Cham: Springer, 2018), 7.

42. Mueller, *Capitalism, Democracy and Ralph's Pretty Good Grocery*.

43. *The Economist*, "The Economist Intelligence Unit's Democracy Index" (updated annually), https://www.eiu.com/topic/democracy-index.

44. A. Solijonov, *Voter Turnout Trends around the World*, Institute for Democracy and Electoral Assistance (IDEA), (2017), 23–33.

45. S. Benhabib, *The Rights of Others* (Cambridge: Cambridge University Press, 2004), 205–207.

46. C. Joppke, "The Evolution of Alien Rights in the United States, Germany and the European Union," in *Citizenship Today*, ed. A. T. Aleinikoff and D. Klusmeyer (Washington, DC: Brookings Institution, 2001), 36–62.

47. D. C. Earnest, "Neither Citizen nor Stranger," *World Politics* 58 (2006): 242.

48. F. Barker and K. McMillan, "Constituting the Democratic Public: New Zealand's Extension of National Voting Rights to Non-citizens," *New Zealand Journal of Public and International Law* 12 (2014): 61.

49. R. Corbett, F. Jacobs, and D. Neville, *The European Parliament*, 9th ed. (London: John Harper, 2016).

50. J. Lichfield, "*Egalité! Liberté! Sexualité!:* Paris, May 1968," *The Independent*, February 23, 2008, https://www.independent.co.uk/news/world/europe/egalit-libert-sexualit-paris-may-1968-784703.html.

FURTHER READING

Abrahamian, A. A. *The Cosmopolites: The Coming of the Global Citizen*. New York: Columbia Global Reports, 2015.

Acosta Arcarazo, D. *The National versus the Foreigner in South America: 200 Years of Migration and Citizenship Law*. Cambridge: Cambridge University Press, 2018.

Aleinikoff, A. T., and D. Klusmeyer. *Citizenship Today*. Washington, DC: Brookings Institution, 2001.

Anderson, B. *Imagined Communities: Reflections on the Origin and Spread of Nationalism*. New York: Verso, 1983.

Archibugi, D. *The Global Commonwealth of Citizens: Toward Cosmopolitan Democracy*. Princeton, NJ: Princeton University Press, 2008.

Bauböck, R. *Democratic Inclusion: Rainer Bauböck in Dialogue*. Manchester: Manchester University Press, 2017.

Bellamy, R. *Citizenship: A Very Short Introduction*. Oxford: Oxford University Press, 2008.

Benhabib, S. *The Rights of Others: Aliens, Residents and Citizens*. Cambridge: Cambridge University Press, 2004.

Berlin, I. "Equality." *Proceedings of the Aristotelian Society* 56 (1955–1956): 301.

Bhabha, J., ed. *Children without a State: A Global Human Rights Challenge*. Cambridge, MA: MIT Press, 2011.

Boll, A. M. *Multiple Nationality and International Law*. Leiden: Martinus Nijhoff, 2007.

Bosniak, L. *The Citizen and the Alien: Dilemmas of Contemporary Membership*. Princeton, NJ: Princeton University Press, 2006.

Bourdieu, P. "The Force of Law." *Hastings Law Journal* 38 (1987): 835.

Brubaker, R. *Citizenship and Nationhood in France and Germany*. Cambridge, MA: Harvard University Press, 1992.

Carens, J. *The Ethics of Immigration*. Oxford: Oxford University Press, 2013.

Cohen, E. F. *Semi-Citizenship in Democratic Politics*. Cambridge: Cambridge University Press, 2009.

Cohen-Eliya, M., and I. Porat. *Proportionality and Constitutional Culture*. Cambridge: Cambridge University Press, 2013.

Cossman, B. *Sexual Citizens: The Legal and Cultural Regulation of Sex and Belonging*. Stanford, CA: Stanford University Press, 2007.

Dahl, R. A. *After the Revolution? Authority in a Good Society*. New Haven, CT: Yale University Press, 1970.

Elden, S. *The Birth of Territory*. Chicago: Chicago University Press, 2013.

Fahrmeir, A. F. "Nineteenth-Century German Citizenships: A Reconsideration." *The Historical Journal* 40 (1997): 721.

Ferrajoli, L. "Dai diritti del cittadino ai diritti della persona." In *La cittadinanza: Appartenenza, identità, diritti*, ed. D. Zolo, 264–268. Rome/Bari: Laterza, 1994.

Habermas, J. *The Postnational Constellation: Political Essays*, trans. M. Pensky. Cambridge: Polity Press, 2001.

Hansen, R. *Citizenship and Immigration in Postwar Britain*. Oxford: Oxford University Press, 2000.

Hany-Lopez, I. *White by Law: The Legal Construction of Race*. New York: NYU Press, 1996.

Harpaz, Y. *Citizenship 2.0: Dual Nationality as a Global Asset*. Princeton, NJ: Princeton University Press, 2019.

Herzog, B. *Revoking Citizenship: Expatriation in America from the Colonial Era to the War on Terror*. New York: NYU Press, 2017.

Howard, M. *The Invention of Peace: Reflections on War and International Order*. New Haven, CT: Yale University Press, 2001.

Isaac, B. H. *The Invention of Racism in Classical Antiquity*. Princeton, NJ: Princeton University Press, 2004.

Ismard, P. *Democracy's Slaves: A Political History of Ancient Greece*, trans. J. M. Todd. Cambridge, MA: Harvard University Press, 2017.

Jessurun d'Oliveira, H. U., ed. *Ontjoodst door de wetenschap. De wetenschappelijke en menselijke integriteit van Arie de Froe onder de bezetting*. Amsterdam: Amsterdam University Press, 2015.

Joppke, C. *Citizenship and Immigration*. Cambridge: Polity Press, 2010.

Kälin, C. Ius Doni *in International Law and EU Law*. Boston: Brill, 2019.

Kamen, D. *Status in Classical Athens*. Princeton, NJ: Princeton University Press, 2013.

Kim, J. *Contested Embrace: Transborder Membership Politics in Twentieth-Century Korea*. Stanford, CA: Stanford University Press, 2016.

Kim, K. *Aliens in Mediaeval Law: The Origins of Modern Citizenship*. Cambridge: Cambridge University Press, 2000.

Kochenov, D. "EU Citizenship without Duties." *European Law Journal* 20 (2014): 482.

Kymlicka, W. *Multicultural Citizenship*. Oxford: Oxford University Press, 1996.

Lohr, E. *Russian Citizenship: From Empire to Soviet Union*. Cambridge, MA: Harvard University Press, 2012.

Manby, B. *Citizenship Law in Africa: A Comparative Study*. New York: Open Society Foundations, 2010.

Mandel, R. *Cosmopolitan Anxieties: Turkish Challenges to Citizenship and Belonging in Germany*. Durham, NC: Duke University Press, 2008.

Marshall, T. H. *Class, Citizenship, and Social Development*. Chicago: University of Chicago Press (1950) 1977.

Milanovic, B. *Global Inequality: A New Approach for the Age of Globalization*. Cambridge, MA: Belknap Press of Harvard University, 2016.

Mueller, J. *Capitalism, Democracy and Ralph's Pretty Good Grocery*. Princeton, NJ: Princeton University Press, 1999.

Müller, I. *Hitler's Justice: The Courts of the Third Reich*. Cambridge, MA: Harvard University Press, 1991.

Munshi, S. "Immigration, Imperialism, and the Legacies of Indian Exclusion," *Yale Journal of Law and Humanities* 28 (2016): 51.

O'Brien, C. *Unity in Adversity: EU Citizenship, Social Justice and the Cautionary Tale of the UK*. Oxford/Portland, OR: Hart Publishing, 2017.

Oakeshott, M. *On Human Conduct*. Oxford: Clarendon Press, 1975.

Oklopcic, Z. *Beyond the People*. Oxford: Oxford University Press, 2018.

Plender, R. *International Migration Law*. Dordrecht: Martinus Nijhoff, 1988.

Pogonyi, S. *Extra-Territorial Ethnic Politics, Discourses and Identities in Hungary*. Cham: Palgrave Macmillan, 2017.

Renan, E. *Qu'est-ce qu'un nation?* Paris: Agora, (1882) 1992.

Saada, M. *Empire's Children: Race, Filiation, and Citizenship in the French Colonies*. Chicago: University of Chicago Press, 2012.

Shachar, A. *The Birthright Lottery: Citizenship and Global Inequality*. Cambridge, MA: Harvard University Press, 2009.

Siedentop, L. *Inventing the Individual: The Origins of Western Liberalism*. Cambridge, MA: Belknap Press of Harvard University, 2014.

Sironi, A. "Nationality of Individuals in Public International Law: A Functional Approach." In *The Changing Role of Nationality in International Law*, ed. A. Annoni and S. Forlati, 54–68. London: Routledge, 2014.

Soysal, Y. N. *Limits of Citizenship: Migrants and Postnational Membership in Europe*. Chicago: University of Chicago Press, 1994.

Spiro, P. J. *At Home in Two Countries: The Past and Future of Dual Citizenship*. New York: NYU Press, 2016.

Štiks, I. *Nations and Citizens in Yugoslavia and Post-Yugoslav States*. London: Bloomsbury Academic, 2015.

Tilly, C. *Coercion, Capital, and European States, AD 990–1992*. Cambridge, MA: Blackwell, 1990.

Torpey, J. *The Invention of the Passport: Surveillance, Citizenship, and the State*. Cambridge: Cambridge University Press, 2000.

Tully, J. *On Global Citizenship: James Tully in Dialogue*. London: Bloomsbury Academic, 2014.

Tully, J. *Strange Multiplicity: Constitutionalism in an Age of Diversity*. Cambridge: Cambridge University Press, 2012.

Varennes, F. de. *Language, Minorities, and Human Rights*. Dordrecht: Kluwer, 1996.

Walzer, M. *Obligations: Essays on Disobedience, War, and Citizenship*. Cambridge, MA: Harvard University Press, 1970.

Weber, E. *Peasants into Frenchmen*. Stanford, CA: Stanford University Press, 1976.

Weil, P. *The Sovereign Citizen: Denaturalization and the Origins of the American Republic*. Philadelphia PA: University of Pennsylvania Press, 2012.

Weis, P. *Nationality and Statelessness in International Law*, 2nd ed. Amsterdam: Sijthoff & Noordhoff, 1979.

Whitman, J. Q. *Hitler's American Model: The United States and the Making of Nazi Race Law*. Princeton, NJ: Princeton University Press, 2017.

INDEX

taxes and, 37, 62, 77, 93
third-tier nationalities and, 128
totalitarianism and, 38–43, 56, 74,
    80–81, 89, 118
travel and, 9–11, 39, 70, 83, 97,
    100–101, 103
United Kingdom and, 37–38, 65–
    67, 76, 81, 86, 94, 98, 108, 112
United States and, 48, 57, 59, 61,
    69, 74, 81, 83–84, 86, 94–95,
    98–107, 112–113
visas and, 6, 8, 10, 14, 72, 76, 83–
    84, 97–98, 101
women and, 63, 79, 88–96, 99
Stewart v. Canada, 255
Štiks, Igor, 111
St. Kitts, 198
St. Paul, xii, 19, 64, 168
Sudan, 182, 219
Sun King, 1
Super-citizenships
    belonging and, 243–244
    birthright and, 244, 250
    Canada and, 243
    children and, 246
    colonialism and, 241, 245
    democracies and, 240, 248
    dignity and, 243, 250
    dissent and, 240, 243, 245
    economic issues and, 249
    education and, 249
    equality and, 243, 251
    ethics and, 246
    European Union (EU) and, 249
    exclusion and, 241, 251
    foreigners and, 250
    freedom and, 240–243, 251
    gap growth of, 249–250
    governance and, 244, 248

hypocrisy and, 240–241, 243, 247,
    252
India and, 249
inequality and, 241, 243
Israel and, 249
justice and, 245, 250
justification of, 243, 248, 251
language and, 241
lotteries and, 241, 250
moral issues and, 251
nationalism and, 243–244, 247
racism and, 245, 247, 251
randomness and, 240–243, 248,
    251–252
self-determination and, 241–242,
    248, 252
sexism and, 245, 247, 251
totalitarianism and, 240–241,
    246–247, 250–251
United States and, 249
Surak, Kristin, 66
Suriname, 137–138
Swastika, 181
Swaziland, 92
Sweden, 136, 163t, 237
Switzerland, 6–7, 11–12, 15, 89,
    117, 119, 173, 201f, 256
Syria, 79, 83, 111, 148
Szobar, Patricia, 26, 184

Tănase v. Moldova, 255
Taney, Justice, 184
Tanganyika, 143
Tanzania, 37, 101
Tarkovsky, Andrei, 181–182
Taxes
    bridal, 93
    duties and, 21, 24, 160, 166–167,
        174, 190

The MIT Press Essential Knowledge Series

DIMITRY KOCHENOV is Professor of EU Constitutional Law and Citizenship at the University of Groningen, the Netherlands. He has held visiting appointments and fellowships at Princeton University (Law and Public Affairs), the College of Europe (Natolin), the University of Turin, NYU Law School (Emile Noël Fellowship), and the Institute for Global Studies (Basel), among other places. He has served as a consultant for governments, law firms, and international institutions, including the Maltese Republic, the Kingdom of the Netherlands, and the European Parliament. He is the author of *EU Enlargement and the Failure of Conditionality*.